AMERICA'S ACHILLES HEEL

Also by the author:

American Apocalypse, an unpublished screenplay

AMERICA'S ACHILLES HEEL

How to Protect Your Family
When America Loses the
Reserve Currency

Elliott J. Schuchardt

National Issues Publishing
First Edition

Copyright © 2025 by Elliott J. Schuchardt. All rights reserved.

No part of this book may be used or reproduced in any manner whatsoever without written permission except in the case of brief quotations embodied in critical articles and reviews. For information contact National Issues Publishing, at access. legal@yahoo.com.

National Issues Publishing books may be purchased for educational, business, or sales promotional use. For information, contact the publisher at the above e-mail address.

The purpose of this book is to discuss public policy in the United States. The author does not provide legal or financial advice. Readers should make their own decisions regarding investments, after consulting a financial adviser.

First edition published August 2025, in Knoxville, Tennessee, by National Issues Publishing.

Tradepaper ISBN: 979-8-218701-64-2
Digital ISBN: 979-8-218744-53-3
Library of Congress Control Number: 2025915667
Printed in the United States of America.

For my sons, Jason and Geoffrey -

So that they will benefit from a nation as strong as the one I found fifty years ago.

Acknowledgments

I would like to express appreciation to several people in connection with this project.

First among these is Dr. Zbigniew Pelcynski, from Pembroke College, at Oxford University. Dr. Pelcynski taught me the importance of questioning the prevailing narratives concerning a political system. Dr. Pelcynski was a refugee from Poland, and was always willing to challenge the prevailing orthodoxy.

I am also grateful to my former Constitutional law professor, Charles Black, from Columbia Law School. From Professor Black, I learned the importance of fighting for social justice, no matter how great the odds.

Dr. Kat Westaway, from Knoxville, Tennessee, provided comments on an accompanying screenplay, which dramatizes the effects of a 75% currency collapse in the United States. Dr. Westaway encouraged me to put these ideas in book form, to provide the facts and theory why such a future could be possible.

Burt Broxterman, an attorney from Albuquerque, New Mexico, served as a mentor during my days of practicing law. Burt was a pillar of integrity in the law, something that is much needed in the profession today.

I am grateful to Naomi Waters for discussing the ideas in this book over many months and years. In many ways, she made the book possible.

Finally, I am grateful to economist Robert Triffin, from Yale University. While I never met Professor Triffin, his dogged determination to publicize the vulnerability of the U.S. dollar served as inspiration to write this book, and to provide this information to a new generation of Americans.

Elliott J. Schuchardt
Knoxville, Tennessee

Table of Contents

Preface 1

Introduction 5

Chapter 1

The De-Industrialization of America 7

Chapter 2

America Has Voluntarily Disarmed 19

    My kingdom for a horse. 22

    America is at war with China in Korea. 24

    America is at war with China over Taiwan. 25

    Covid-19 reveals cracks in the system. 26

    Empty arsenals. 29

    Empty shipyards. 34

    Empty textile mills. 37

    My kingdom for a computer chip. 41

    Falling behind in the space race. 45

    Rare earth minerals – China's grip on the U.S. 48

    America's import reliance on critical materials. 51

    America's food vulnerability. 53

    The U.S. economy is hollowed out. 55

Chapter 3

This Ship Will Sink 61

    Federal budget deficit. 68

Trade deficit 74

  America for sale 78

  U.S. Foreign Currency Reserves are Dwindling 82

Chapter 4

Dueling Views of The Dollar 91

  The gold standard v. the urge to print 92

  Bretton Woods -- the New Gold Standard 98

  Robert Triffin sounds the alarm. 100

  Robert Roosa pitches the reserve currency. 103

  France objects to the gold pool. 104

  Triffin returns to Europe. 108

Chapter 5

The New Gold Standard – the Petrodollar 111

  The petrodollar – by the numbers. 118

  De-industrialization begins. 121

  Pittsburgh – harbinger of economic collapse. 124

  The World War II generation fights back. 126

  Stockpiling 128

  Strategic Grain Reserve 129

  Strategic Petroleum Reserve. 129

  Civil Defense Preparation 130

  1985 -- The Plaza Accord 130

  Protection of the auto industry. 131

  Efforts to avoid currency manipulation. 133

CONTENTS

1992 -- the turning point in American politics 135

The baby boomers sell the crown jewels. 139

North American Free Trade Agreement. 140

Liquidation of Strategic Grain Reserve. 142

Sale of the Strategic Petroleum Reserve. 142

Liquidation of National Defense Stockpiles. 144

Sale of American Technology. 144

The China shock. 145

Strong dollar – weak United States. 151

Chapter 6
The New Confederacy 157

Chapter 7
Defending the Dollar 163

Iraq threatens the dollar. 168

Libya threatens the dollar. 171

Venezuela threatens the dollar. 173

America is vulnerable. 174

Chapter 8
Countermeasures – BRICS 175

Russia sells its treasury bonds. 177

The rise of BRICS. 181

Chapter 9
Defending the Kingdom With Tariffs 187

The United States lowers its tariffs. 190

Trump sounds the alarm. 190

Trump keeps the petrodollar in place. 191

Chapter 10

Consequences 193

Thailand – 1997 195

Russia -- 1998 197

Argentina -- 2001 198

Zimbabwe -- 2007 199

The United States is vulnerable. 200

Chapter 11

Premonitions of disaster 205

Titanic Redux 206

Premonitions of Economic Collapse 210

Chapter 12

Solutions 217

Lessons from the British pound. 220

Lessons for the United States. 225

National Goals 226

Chapter 13

How to Protect Your Family 229

Barter items 230

Remote real estate in the United States 231

Stockpiling food 232

Prepper conventions and podcasts 234

CONTENTS

Precious metals 235
Bitcoin and crypto currency. 237
Domestic foreign currency accounts. 237
Online foreign exchange accounts. 239
Offshore bank accounts. 240
Tactical relocation overseas 242
Foreign residency 243
Foreign real estate 245
Conclusion 247
About the Author 249
Bibliography 251

Preface

The first rule of self defense is situational awareness.

This book argues that the United States is ignoring a material risk to our nation. In other words, we lack situational awareness.

For the past 75 years, Americans have grown accustomed to a lifestyle that far exceeds the standard of living for much of the planet.

We enjoy our suburban houses, shopping malls and cars. It is easy to assume that America will always have these things. Our leaders tell us that "the United States is strong," "the dollar is secure," and "the people are safe."

It is time to take a hard look at these phrases, and see whether they are still true.

This book argues that American "prosperity" is increasingly an illusion, created by our nation's military control over the oil fields in the Middle East. This military dominance gives the United States a partial monopoly on the sale of oil. Many oil producers will only sell oil for U.S. dollars.

The oil monopoly creates artificial demand for the dollar. In other words, people are forced to buy dollars, because they need oil. If a foreign country needs to purchase a billion dollars of oil, they can't do so with Japanese yen, or Indian rupees, or euro. They must first acquire U.S. dollars for the transaction.

To get the dollars, the buyer of oil must first sell goods to the United States. We end up with a billion dollars of Vietnamese rice or Chinese goods, and pay with only printed dollars. Under the existing system, we get the goods for free, because we provide nothing in return, other than printed dollars. Thus, our currency is artificially sustained by means of the oil monopoly.

This pricing system is known as the petrodollar. The petrodollar fills our nation's shopping malls with imported goods, and our grocery stores with imported foods. We are prosperous because we are selling dollars to the world. These dollars have value because they are convertible to oil from the Middle East.

What would happen if the United States did not have the oil monopoly? In other words, if Saudi Arabia were to sell oil for a currency other than the dollar – would the rest of the world still need to purchase our currency?

This book argues that the U.S. dollar is unstable. Our currency could lose much of its value overnight, if the Middle East were to trade oil for a different currency. If this were to happen, the United States could be plunged into poverty in a short period of time.

The world is putting together an alliance – known as BRICS – which will have the power to replace the dollar for trading oil, and other commodities. When BRICS is ready, it could replace the dollar with its own currency, which the United States will not be able to print. This could be a "turn key" operation, requiring no military action.

In other words, the United States has an Achilles heel.

In Greek mythology, Achilles was a hero of the Trojan War. Achilles was known to be invulnerable, because his mother dipped him in the river Styx when he was a child. The water from the river allegedly protected Achilles' body from any kind of injury. However, Achilles wasn't protected on his heel, because his mother held Achilles by his heel when she dipped him in the water. As a result, the mighty Achilles could be killed by means of an injury to his heel. That, in fact, is how he died in the Trojan War. The Greek legend gives us the phrase, Achilles heel – meaning a hidden vulnerability.

Americans need to know that their standard of living is vulnerable. Our ability to purchase Japanese cars, Mexican produce and Chinese goods could collapse in the near future, if we lose our ability to sell Middle East oil for dollars.

This book aims to promote "situational awareness" of the dollar's weakness. It identifies the risk to America's economy and military security, and proposes solutions for the problems.

PREFACE

Finally, it offers suggestions on how to protect your family and assets, for when America loses the reserve currency.

Introduction

In the closing days of World War II, the victorious allied powers competed for whatever advantages they could obtain from the remains of Nazi Germany.

The United States and Russia searched Germany for scientists who understood the secrets of the V-2 rocket. The Soviet Union dismantled German factories, and shipped the tools back to Russia. Britain and France used German prisoners of war to work on farms and rebuild their economies. Soviet soldiers took their own war prizes, and raped an estimated two million women following the fall of Berlin.

However, it was the United States that ended up with the greatest war prize of all. In 1944, in negotiations with the British empire, the United States gained control of the world's reserve currency.

This was no small feat. In the years leading up to World War II, Britain controlled 25% of the earth's land mass. Empire brought tremendous advantages to Britain. These included the ability to exclude other countries from British colonies. It also included the ability to insist that trade be done solely in British pounds, which the United Kingdom could print at will.

In 1944, the power to create the world's primary reserve currency shifted to the United States. This event occurred in a small town in New Hampshire, called Bretton Woods.

The shift in the reserve currency gave the United States almost unlimited power to create wealth essentially out of thin air. It was – and remains as of this date – an Aladdin's lamp capable of placing armies anywhere on the globe with a minimum of effort and resources committed by the United States.

As we will see in this book, the lamp is a two-edged sword. While the reserve currency has brought enormous wealth to the United States, it has also eviscerated large parts of the United States economy. This is because the dollar is artificially overvalued. An overvalued dollar is dangerous for two reasons. First, it hurts our nation's industries by making the United States expensive, and uncompetitive. Second, an overvalued currency will eventually return to its true market value. In other words, the dollar can collapse, creating havoc for everything that it touches.

This book tells the story of how we got here, and offers suggestions on how best to move forward.

CHAPTER 1
The De-Industrialization of America

The United States used to be a very different place.

At the end of World War II, the United States was unrivalled on the planet. Our steel mills were the arsenal of democracy. Our factories produced electronics, metal products, textiles and vehicles. The United States had a monopoly on atomic weapons, and was the dominant scientific power in every field.

When I was young -- in the early 1970s -- my mother told me that our family was lucky to be living in the United States. She showed me a globe, and pointed out where we lived. My mother didn't study economics. However, she knew that there were wars elsewhere on the planet. And she knew that we were safe in Ohio, far from conflict and famine.

In retrospect, it turns out that southern Ohio was the place to be in 1971. We were living in the center of a vast industrial economy, that spread out across the American Midwest. Our nation's leaders had carefully nurtured this economy for years.

It had only been a few decades since the Wright Brothers had experimented with airplanes in Dayton, Ohio – not far from our home.

In 1905, Wilbur Wright flew the world's first airplane for a record-breaking 39 minutes in Dayton. This event marked the inception of modern aviation. And it happened not far from where I lived.

To our north, Cleveland, was a major automotive center. In 1931, the city boasted more than 80 different carmakers. In 1970, Cleveland was second to Detroit, in the percentage of its workers engaged in the automobile industry. Companies such as Warner & Swasey and Cleveland Twist Drill made lathes, planers and drill presses that were essential for making cars.

Cleveland was also the site of advanced research and development. During World War II, Pratt & Whitney and General Electric developed jet engines in Cleveland. GE also pioneered radar technology there.

Other companies contributed to the war effort. Cleveland Graphite Bronze Company made aircraft bearings; Alcoa developed advanced metals; and Case Institute of Technology developed synthetic rubber.

North of Cleveland lay Detroit itself. In Detroit, Ford Motor Company operated the largest factory in the world. The factory, known as the River Rouge complex, produced everything that was necessary to produce a car, from the raw materials to the finished product. The factory included a blast furnace, steel mill, glass plant, cement plant, power plant, as well as the car factory. At its peak, River Rouge employed tens of thousands of workers.

To our west lay Cincinnati. Cincinnati was the home of the Crossley Corporation, which literally invented the refrigerator. Crossley was also the first company in the world to mass produce radios. During the Second World War, Crosley produced remote-controlled bomb fuses for the military. At its peak, the company produced more 16,500 fuses every day – an astonishing number. With more than 10,000 employees, Crossley was the largest employer in Cincinnati.

To our northeast, lay Pittsburgh, Pennsylvania. In 1970, Pittsburgh's rivers were lined with steel mills, producing steel for the car industry and the nation's military. In Pittsburgh, U.S. Steel operated the largest steel mill in the world, at its Homestead plant. Jones & Laughlin employed over 20,000 steel workers in Alliquippa.

During World War II, Pittsburgh produced over 95 million tons of steel. This steel went into ships, aircraft carriers and guns of every sort. On Neville Island, the American Bridge Corporation produced landing craft for the war. Altogether, Pittsburgh produced over 20% of the landing craft used during the war. North of Pittsburgh, Butler produced jeeps.

In 1970, Pittsburgh had the third largest collection of Fortune 500 companies in America. Pittsburgh was the home of United States Steel (then the largest producer of steel in the world); Alcoa Aluminum (the world's largest producer of aluminum); Westinghouse Electric (which produced nuclear power plants); and Pittsburgh Plate Glass.

Closer to my home, in Logan, Ohio, Goodyear employed 600 people making instrument panels for the auto industry. Goodyear was important to the Ohio economy. During World War II, Goodyear ranked 30th of all defense companies, nationwide, in the value of goods manufactured for the war. In 1970, Goodyear employed 7,600 workers in Akron, Ohio alone. In that year, Goodyear made the first tires to land on the moon, as part of the Apollo 14 program.

Forty miles to our southeast, lay the small town of Portsmouth, Ohio. In 1970, Portsmouth enriched uranium for the nation's nuclear weapons program. My family always discussed the atomic plant in hushed tones. It was illegal to even take pictures of the facility.

The production in Ohio, Pennsylvania and Michigan was a small fraction of the activity in the United States during World War II. In just a few years, the United States produced two million trucks, 9,000 warships, 151 aircraft carriers, 86,000 tanks, 193,000 artillery pieces, and 297,000 aircraft. In addition, the United States produced millions of uniforms, boots, tents, cots, helmets and tons of food. All of this was necessary to supply an army that peaked at 12 million people in 1945.

How things have changed. Today, much of this industry is gone. Cleveland's machine tool company, Warner & Swasey, closed in 1992. In Cincinnati, the giant ten-story factory of the Crosley Corporation is abandoned, and now sits in ruins.

In Detroit, much of the River Rouge complex is now closed and underused. The power plant closed in 2021. Nine hundred acres of the site are now a historic landmark. Parts of the plant are still running. However, today, the River Rouge site generally assembles parts made elsewhere, or outside of the country.

The Goodyear plant in Logan, Ohio closed in 1999. Goodyear also closed much of its tire manufacturing in Akron, Ohio. Goodyear's employees in Akron fell from 7,600, in 1970, to 2,600 today. In July 2024, Goodyear announced that it was moving an additional 175 jobs to Costa Rica.

The atomic plant in Portsmouth, Ohio closed in 2001. Today, the massive gaseous diffusion plant is abandoned, and is being cleaned up by the Department of Energy.

Pittsburgh went through a massive economic collapse in the 1980s – losing hundreds of thousands of jobs. The city's longtime employer, Jones & Laughlin, merged with another steel company in the mid-1980s, and today no longer exists.

The nation's largest steelmaker – United States Steel – is today a fraction of its former size. In 2025, the company was sold to a Japanese steel company, because the United States no longer had the money or the technology to operate the company efficiently.

Alliquippa – which formerly boasted 20,000 steelworkers – is now abandoned. The site of the former mill is a now an overgrown, grassy field. All that remains of the factory is a historical marker sign.

On the south side of the Allegheny River, the steel mills operated by U.S. Steel and Jones & Laughlin are now gone. During the 1980s, the mills were dismantled, and blown up with dynamite. Today, the sprawling mills in Homestead and on the Southside are shopping malls, selling foreign-made goods.

East of Pittsburgh, in Braddock, there is an abandoned Catholic Church, built in 1901. The church is surrounded by a largely abandoned community.

The destruction of Ohio's economy in the last fifty years is a microcosm of what was happening elsewhere in the United States. In 1970, about 18 million people worked in manufacturing in our country. That was about a quarter of all jobs in the United States.

Today, far fewer people work in manufacturing. This poses a problem for the United States. Our nation is growing weaker. We are not just losing jobs. We are losing national security, because increasingly we cannot produce basic goods.

For the past thirty years, our nation's leaders have intentionally de-industrialized the United States. In 1994, President Bill Clinton pushed through the North American Free Trade Agreement (NAFTA). That agreement eliminated tariffs between the United States and Mexico. The agreement encouraged American corporations to shift production, and jobs, to Mexico.

Later, the United States started shifting jobs to China. This was done at the request of America's largest companies. In 2000, the CEOs of more than 340 companies, including General Motors, IBM, Boeing, McDonald Douglas, and Caterpillar argued that the United States should grant permanent favorable tariff status to China.

The Clinton administration granted their request. In October 2000, Congress passed legislation granting China permanent access to America's most preferential tariff rates. Between October 2000 and

April 30, 2001, more than eighty corporations announced that they intended to shift production from the United States to China.

In the years that followed, the United States industrial base collapsed. Since 1998, the United States has closed over 80,000 factories. In 1977, the United States had 192 manufacturing facilities that employed more than 5,000 people. By 2007, that number had dropped to only 49.

In just ten years, between 2000 and 2010, the United States lost over one-third of its manufacturing jobs. Manufacturing employment in the United States fell from approximately 18 million workers in 2000, to a low of 11.5 million, in January 2010. And just like that, seven million jobs disappeared from the United States.

Today, only 15% of the population of Ohio is engaged in manufacturing. Compared to the rest of the United States, this is actually a high number. In Tennessee, only 13% of the population works in manufacturing. The percentage is much lower in other states. For example, the number is only 4% in New York, 7% in Virginia, 5% in Florida, and 4% in Nevada.

The decision to outsource American manufacturing destroyed more than just factory jobs. Entire communities were wiped out.

In order to survive, a community of people needs a source of income. That income can come – for example – from the sale of agricultural products (as in Iowa), the sale of financial services (as in New York City), the sale of television advertising (as in Los Angeles) or from the sale of machine tools (as was the case in Ohio). When that source of income is disrupted, the entire community suffers.

Our nation also lost the ability to make things. This is important for national defense.

Since 1970, American steel production has declined by 30%. We now make less steel than we did fifty years ago, despite large increases in the world's population. In 1970, the United States was the world's top producer of aluminum. Today, our aluminum production is down by 80%.

America's auto industry is also reduced. In the last fifty years, America's car manufacturers shifted large portions of their production to Mexico. After the passage of NAFTA, America's auto manufacturers moved 360,000 out of 390,000 jobs from the Detroit region. Entire neighborhoods were bulldozed, as a result. The only surviving structures were the brick churches, built in the early 20th century.

Today, at least 47% of the cars sold in the United States are now imported. However, the numbers are worse than that. No car sold in the United States is made entirely in the United States. The auto factories that remain are largely assembly plants, which assemble imported parts. Of the cars that are allegedly "made in the USA," at least 30% of the parts are produced outside the United States. Thus, the percentage of American-made cars is significantly lower than half of the cars sold in the United States.

Increasingly, the American people cannot afford a new car. Car sales in the United States are now lower than in 1986 – nearly forty years ago. This has occurred, even though the U.S. population has increased by more than 20%.

In May 2025, the average age of a passenger vehicle in the United States hit a record of 14.5 years. This is a big change. In 1970, when America dominated car manufacturing, the average age of a car in the United States was only 4.9 years. Imagine getting a new car every few years. It used to be that way, when cars were made locally with American-made parts.

The average age of a car in the United States began to increase in the 1970s and 80s with improvements in quality. However, the number is also affected by the affordability of a vehicle. In 1993, when Clinton started moving factories to Mexico, the average age of a new car in the United States was 8.3 years. In other words, since the passage of NAFTA, Americans are keeping their vehicles 75% longer – an increase of six years.

Other areas have declined, as well. For example, consider consumer electronics. In 1966, 100,000 people in the United States made televisions, radios and consumer electronics. Today, the United States produces virtually no consumer electronics. Virtually all cell phones are imported. The United States produces virtually no flat screen televisions.

We see similar declines in America's textile industry. In 1970, the United States employed over two million people, making textiles. At that time, Fort Payne, Alabama was known as the Sock Capital of the World. In the 1990s, Fort Payne had 120 mills, that employed 7,500 workers. Today, Fort Payne's mills are closed. The city produces almost no clothing. Employment in the American textile industry has declined by more than 80%.

As of 2025, American manufacturing continues to decline. The Institute for Supply Management (ISM) maintains an index that shows whether American manufacturing is expanding or contracting. If the number is above 50, then manufacturing in the United States is expanding. If the number is below 50, then manufacturing is contracting.

As of June 2024, the ISM index showed that American manufacturing was contracting. For the prior 32 months, the index has shown 30 months of contraction. Thus, we are looking at a systemic problem.

This book argues that American manufacturing is declining because the United States is not competitive. Our currency – the U.S. dollar – is simply too expensive. It is cheaper for our companies – and foreign competition – to manufacture goods offshore, and import goods to the United States.

We are now dependent upon a sea of imported goods. In 2024, the United States imported hundreds of billions of dollars of foreign-made goods, leaving our nation with a trade deficit of $1 trillion per year. We are dependent upon foreigners to supply us with auto parts, cell phones, televisions, cameras, textiles, and machinery of all sorts. Even worse, we are dependent upon foreigners for much of our food supply. Reportedly, half of the vegetables sold in the United States are imported.

Our former industrialized society has been hollowed out, and has been replaced by a seamless web of shopping malls, consuming imported goods. Coast-to-coast, our nation is known for consumption. Our nation is no longer known for steel mills and factories exporting to the world. Instead, America is now dominated by Walmart, Best Buy, Home Depot, and Lowes – selling imported goods from coast to coast.

A list of the largest employers in Ohio shows just how weak that state's economy has become, in terms of actual production. According to the Ohio Department of Development, the largest employers in Ohio are as follows:

Table 1.1

Ohio Largest Employers

Rank	Company	Number of Employees	Industry
1.	Cleveland Clinic Foundation	56,986	Health
2.	Walmart	55,262	Retail
3.	Amazon	45,000	Retail
4.	Kroger Co.	44,077	Retail: Food

5.	Ohio State University and Medical Center	35,656	Education & Health
6.	University Hospitals Health System	30,891	Health
7.	Mercy Health Partners	30,510	Health
8.	OhioHealth	30,488	Health
9.	Wright Patterson Air Force Base	28,000	
10.	JP Morgan Chase	20,228	Finance
11.	ProMedica	18,712	Health
12.	Giant Eagle	17,400	Retail: Food
13.	Cincinnati Children's Hospital Medical Center	17,204	Health
14.	FedEx	15,250	Air Delivery
15.	United Parcel Service	15,236	Air Delivery
16.	Kettering Health	14,413	Health
17.	Lowe's Companies	14,400	Retail
18.	Honda Motor Co.	14,400	Manufacture: Motor Vehicles
19.	Home Depot	12,600	Retail
20.	Target	12,410	Retail

The above list should concern any person living in the United States. Rather than making useful products – such as cars, motors, and electronics -- our nation's economy now consumes wealth.

Nine of the top twenty employers in Ohio are engaged in consumption. These are Walmart, Amazon, Kroger, Giant Eagle, Lowe's, Home Depot, Target, Federal Express and UPS. These names are not just names that we see on the highway. These names have become the core of the United States economy.

The balance of Ohio's economy doesn't provide much comfort. Eight of the twenty largest companies in Ohio provide healthcare. While there is a place for hospitals and doctors, 40% of Ohio's economy is generating no wealth at all.

Of the remaining companies – JP Morgan Chase, Wright Patterson Air Force Base, and Honda Motor Company – only one, Honda, is arguably engaged in manufacturing.

According to the U.S. Bureau of Economic Analysis, 68% of the U.S. economy is consumption. This statistic is demonstrated by the largest employers in the United States – companies that help our nation consume the world's goods.

Astonishingly, economists do not consider consumption when comparing the economies of nations. In the United States, our economists claim that consumption is a "product," that should be counted as part of gross domestic product. They claim that we are a "rich nation," because we consume more products than our adversaries, such as China and Russia.

This book disagrees. Consumption is very different from production. A person delivering potato chips is not the same as a person making computer chips. When we adjust our numbers, and exclude consumption, we will find that the American economy is far smaller than what our economists claim.

Are you starting to get my drift? Our nation – the mighty United States – is no longer as strong and powerful as we were in the Second World War – or even as were 50 years ago – in 1970. We have sold the machine tools and the technology to other nations. We have closed our factories, and replaced them with shopping malls.

All of this has occurred because of how the world economy is set up.

For fifty years, the reserve currency has been an enormous blessing to the United States. However, the reserve currency has created a dangerous dependence in America today. Our nation is dependent upon a single product to obtain overseas goods -- the export of United States dollars. However, these dollars may not have value overseas in the near future.

In this book, I argue that the United States has become a paper tiger. In other words, the United States can be militarily defeated by a few events that could occur solely on paper, with a handful of foreign signatures. As explained below, these events are already in motion.

CHAPTER 2
America Has Voluntarily Disarmed

The Japanese have a saying that goes "rich nation, strong army." In Japan, this is more than a slogan. It has been the country's official policy for nearly two hundred years. It is worth taking a look at the Japanese experience, to understand why.

Prior to 1850, Japan had a stratified society. The emperor was at the top. He was protected by a warrior class, known as the samurai. Beneath the samurai were the merchants and peasants. Japan's leaders were not open to foreign ideas. They pursued a policy of isolationism, and sought to keep the "barbarians" out of the country.

Meanwhile, other countries learned new technologies. While Japan was hiding behind isolationism, the United States and Western Europe were learning how to make steel, ships, gun powder, guns, and glass. The West learned the secrets of steam and electricity. As a result, by 1850, Western Europe and the United States were far ahead of Japan, technologically.

In the mid-1850s, the two systems came into conflict. On July 8, 1853, four American navy vessels, under the command of Commodore Matthew Perry, sailed into Tokyo harbor, in Japan. Perry's mission was to establish trade between the United States and Japan.

Perry brought with him a variety of gifts for the Japanese emperor. These included a working model of a steam locomotive, a telescope, a telegraph, and a variety of wines and liquors from the West. These were intended to convince the Japanese of the superiority of Western culture. In the event the Japanese were reluctant to do business, Perry also brought with him canon and plenty of guns.

On that first visit, Perry delivered a letter from President Fillmore, asking the Japanese to trade with the United States. After conveying his request, Perry left Tokyo for several months.

The following year, Perry returned to Tokyo with an even larger squadron of ships to receive the emperor's answer. The Japanese emperor grudgingly accepted Perry's demands. On March 31, 1854, Japan and the United States signed the Treaty of Kanagawa. In the treaty, Japan agreed to open two ports for refueling and provisioning of American ships. Japan also agreed to protect stranded American sailors.

Admiral Perry's visit to Tokyo harbor was a wake-up call to the Japanese. The Japanese learned that they were years behind the West in terms of military technology. After 1854, Japan embarked a crash course of learning from the West and industrializing its economy. Japan began to hire foreign experts to learn the West's secrets.

The Japanese government brought in hundreds of Western experts to jump start Japanese industry. In the mid-1870s, Japan had over 500 foreign specialists working in the country.

These specialists helped Japan set up factories in the shipping industry, agriculture and manufacturing. In the industrial sector, Japan set up the Shinagawa Glass Factory, the Tomioka Silk Mill, the Aichi Spinning Mill, the Fukagawa Cement Works, and Sapporo Brewery.

In 1872, Japan set up its first railroad between Tokyo and Yokohama. Britain provided the railway cars, financing, and the chief civil engineer, Edmund Morel. In 1874, Japan opened a second line between Kobe and Osaka. By 1900, a network of rail lines spread across Japan.

These experts were expensive by Japanese standards. At a time when the Japanese head minister of state was earning 800 yen per month, the British engineer, Thomas Kinder, received a monthly salary of 1,045 yen, for his work at the imperial mint. The pay difference shows the importance of Western technology to Japan.

By 1877, Japan was in a position to begin exporting its own manufactured goods. In that year, the Japanese Home Ministry organized its first Domestic Industrial Exposition. At the expo, Japan displayed 84,000 products in six categories, including machinery and agriculture. The expo was successful, attracting 450,000 visitors over three months.

As a result of this work, Japan was able to rapidly build up its army. Japan was able to successfully resist European colonists in the late 19th century. Instead of being a victim of Western colonization, Japan was able to colonize its weaker neighbors, and fight the Western powers on their own terms.

In 1904, Japan went to war with the Russian empire, in what is now northeastern China. By the end of 1904, the Japanese navy had sunk every ship in Russia's Pacific fleet. Japan also occupied the Russian naval base of Port Arthur, located near present-day Shanghai.

Russia sought to reinforce its eastern territories by sending its Baltic fleet from St. Petersburg – located in northwestern Russia – to Asia, to defend Vladivostok. This was a voyage of nearly 20,000 nautical miles -- a huge undertaking in the early 1900s.

On May 27, 1905, the Japanese engaged the Russian fleet at the Tsushima Straits, located between Korea and southwestern Japan. By the end of the next day, the Japanese had sunk eight Russian battleships – a loss of more than 5,000 men for the Russians. Only three Russian vessels made it to Vladivostok.

On September 5, 1905, Russia and Japan concluded the war with the Treaty of Portsmouth. Under the terms of the treaty, Russia ceded Port Arthur to the Japanese. Japan also gained control of Manchuria and the Korean peninsula. This set the stage for Japan's later seizure of territory in China, at the beginning of World War II.

Japan's victory over Russia in 1905 stunned the Western world. The siege of Port Arthur during the war introduced many technologies used in subsequent wars. These included howitzers, the first fully-automatic machine gun, bolt-action magazine rifles, barbed wire entanglements, electric fences, searchlights, hand grenades, and tactical radio signaling.

Japan could not have done this without its rapid industrialization in the late 19th century. By rapidly industrializing, Japan effectively defended its homeland, and was able to expand its area of control well beyond the Japanese islands.

Fifty years later, on July 14, 1901, Japan erected a statute of American Commodore Perry at the spot where Perry first landed in Japan. The monument survived World War II and is now the centerpiece of a small seaside park in Yokosuka, Japan.

Thus, Japan shows the importance of the ability to make products, in national defense. Other countries, such as Germany, have a similar philosophy.

My kingdom for a horse.

In the 13th century, the Germans began to recite a proverb about the importance of military planning. The proverb went like this:

> The wise tell us that a nail keeps a shoe; a shoe a horse;
> a horse a man, a man a castle, that can fight.

This proverb has been repeated many times over the years, and in many languages. In 1629, a clergyman -- Thomas Adams -- described the aphorism as follows:

> The want of a nayle looseth the shooe,
> The losse of shooe troubles the horse,
> The horse indangereth the rider,

> The rider breaking his ranke molests the company,
> So farre as to hazard the whole army.

In other words, the loss of a single nail is sufficient to endanger an entire army. A more modern version of the aphorism goes as follows:

> For want of a nail, the shoe was lost.
> For want of a shoe, the horse was lost.
> For want of a horse, the rider was lost.
> For want of a rider, the message was lost.
> For want of a message, the battle was lost.
> For want of a battle, the kingdom was lost.
> And all for the want of a horseshoe nail.

Shakespeare dramatized this idea in Richard III. At the end of the play, King Richard has lost his horse on the battlefield. Richard's opponent, Richmond, is also on the battlefield, searching for Richard. Richard cries out, "A horse, a horse! My kingdom for a horse!" At that point, it is too late. Richard dies shortly thereafter.

This idea -- that a single nail -- can make a difference in a battle has been taught to military commanders for nearly a thousand years.

Nevertheless, America's military planners seem to have missed the lesson. Increasingly, America doesn't seem to care where its military supplies come from.

For example, let's consider whether the United States can make a nail.

In 2013 the United States consumed 629,716 tons of steel nails. Eighty percent of those nails were manufactured outside of the United States, and imported. Two-thirds of the imported nails came from five countries: China (28%), Taiwan (16%), Korea (11%), UAE (6%), and Vietnam (6%).

If America's consumption of nails were to be melted down and cast into a single block of steel, that block would cover an area the size of a football field, to a depth of 45 feet.

Now -- in your mind's eye -- remove 80% of that football field of steel. Those are nails that the United States does not -- and cannot -- produce. Domestic production of nails will only get America to the twenty yard line. Asia controls 80% of that field. For America, its game over, in terms of nail production.

Multiply this lack of productive capacity by hundreds of thousands of products, and you begin to get a sense of America's vulnerability.

Every year, the software company, Govini, publishes a National Security Scorecard. The scorecard is a report on the security of America's defense supply chain. In the report, Govini looks at foreign ownership of "Tier 1 suppliers." Tier 1 suppliers are the principal subcontractors for American companies that make weapons.

In its 2025 report, Govini found that only 37% of the Pentagon's Tier 1 suppliers were located in the United States. In other words, the United States has outsourced more than 60% of our military production. Even worse, Govini found that nearly 10% of our nation's Tier 1 suppliers are located in China.

That is a problem for the United States, because our country is at war with China in at least two different conflicts. Let's briefly consider some history.

America is at war with China in Korea.

On June 25, 1950, North Korea invaded South Korea. The United States deployed about 300,000 troops to Korea, to oppose the invasion.

By the end of 1950, the United States thought that it had won the war. The United States steadily advanced, and moved into North Korea. Soldiers began to talk about the possibility of being home for Christmas. They were premature.

In November 1950, China launched a large scale attack on United States forces in North Korea. Chinese forces swept out of China, and pushed the United States back towards the 38th parallel, which divided the country before the war. For the balance of the war, China had about 1.3 million soldiers in Korea.

On July 27, 1953, North and South Korea entered into an armistice. The agreement created a demilitarized zone along the 38th parallel. Since then, North and South Korea have maintained a tense stand-off along what has become known as the "DMZ."

Most Americans think that the Korean war is over. However, the armistice did not end the war. The agreement was only a cease-fire. Thus, the United States is currently engaged in an active war with China, for control over the Korean peninsula.

It is easy to say that the situation in Korea is stabilized. Neither the United States nor China has any interest in disturbing the status quo in Korea. However, the United States is also engaged in a second war with China – this time, over Taiwan.

America is at war with China over Taiwan.

After World War II, two armies fought for control of China. These were the Nationalists, led by Chiang Kai-shek, and the Communist forces, led by Mao Zedong.

During the war, the United States assisted the Nationalist government. The United States equipped and trained 60 divisions of soldiers, on behalf of Chiang Kai-shek. In 1948, the United States provided an additional $400 million in aid to the Nationalist government.

The United States viewed this as good policy, because Chiang Kai-shek claimed to be opposed to the Communists. However, Chiang Kai-shek was not a popular leader. Most Chinese viewed him as a puppet of foreign powers. They also viewed him as a dictator, who did not respect human rights.

In 1949, the Communist forces, led by Mao Zedong, entered Shanghai, and proclaimed the People's Republic of China. America's allies – the defeated Nationalists -- fled China, together with China's gold reserves. They set up a government on an island that is now known as Taiwan. Since 1949, Taiwan has claimed to be the true government for all of China. Similarly, the Communist forces in Beijing have claimed to be the proper government for all of China, including Taiwan.

In America, it is common to think that the Chinese civil war is over. However, that is not the case. Since 1949, the United States has continued to provide military aid to the Nationalist forces, encamped in Taiwan. Mainland China views the Nationalist forces as nothing more than a rebel army, protected by a foreign power – the United States.

At times, the ongoing civil war between mainland China and Taiwan has erupted in active fighting. During the 1950s, the Peoples Republic of China periodically shelled the outer islands of Taiwan. In 1958, President Eisenhower threatened to use nuclear weapons against China, to stop the fighting.

As of 2025, the People's Republic of China continues to view Taiwan as Chinese soil. The United States does not respect the Chinese view. The United States continues to provide military aid to Taiwan, as part of the ongoing war. It is estimated that the Pentagon maintains at least 500 military personnel in Taiwan.

Thus, when the United States ships factories to China, that's the same thing as shipping a jeep factory to Hitler during World War II, and asking the Germans to make jeeps for the United States. The idea is foolish and nonsensical. Yet, the United States has done exactly that.

Since 2000, the United States has shipped more than just a jeep factory to China. The United States has shipped a substantial portion of its industrial base to China.

Covid-19 reveals cracks in the system.

The covid pandemic revealed significant problems in the nation's supply chain. In early 2020, health care officials projected that covid-19 could affect up to 40% of the United States population, with over four million people requiring intensive-care (ICU) level treatment over time.

It was thought that as many as 300,000 people could require ICU beds simultaneously.

Government officials urgently proclaimed the need for ventilators. In early 2020, the United States had approximately 62,000 ventilators available. This was far fewer than the amount thought necessary. In March 2020, the New York Times reported that the United States might need as many as one million ventilators to deal with the pandemic. The U.S. government ordered the manufacture of nearly 200,000 ventilators, to be delivered by end of the year.

Government officials soon discovered that the United States did not have the ability to produce such machines. During the prior two decades, American ventilator companies had outsourced production of the machines to Asia. Efforts to import the machines were generally not successful, because foreign countries were prioritizing their own populations for production.

The U.S. government considered this matter to be a national emergency. The Trump Administration invoked the Defense Production Act to encourage automotive manufacturers to partner with ventilator companies to speed domestic production.

The covid emergency demonstrated the limits of America's industrial base. By October 2020, the United States was only able to produce about 15,000 ICU-level ventilators. By that time, the government learned that it would need far fewer ventilators, and reduced the order.

It is useful to compare U.S. production of ventilators to that of China, during the same period. At the beginning of the pandemic, in March 2020, China had eight companies producing ventilators. These companies produced ventilators for about 20% of global demand. Collectively, they could produce about 2,200 ventilators per week. During a single month -- March 2020 -- China produced and exported 16,000 ventilators. This was more than the United States was able to produce in the next eight months.

The United States also had difficulty supplying simpler products, such as face masks. During the covid pandemic, demand for N-95 face masks soared. In a normal month, there is limited demand for N-95 masks. They are typically only worn by healthcare personnel, in a hospital setting. Now, in March 2020, the U.S. government recommended that the entire population wear face masks, for the duration of the epidemic.

As with ventilators, the United States was not prepared. In the early 2000s, the United States had outsourced virtually all of its production of face masks to Asia. By 2020, fewer than 10% of American N95 mask consumption was produced in the United States. As a result, the United States was not able to meet demand with domestic production, when demand soared with the epidemic. At the beginning of the epidemic, the United States was forced to rely upon home-made, hand-stitched masks because the United States could not acquire foreign-made masks.

The covid years were a wake-up call to America's business community. For years, America's Fortune 500 executives had been crowing about their supply chain management. They considered themselves "geniuses," because they were able to close factories in Ohio, Indiana and Illinois, and move the production facilities to Mexico, and then to China. Products that were formerly manufactured and sold for dollars, could now be manufactured for pennies, but still be sold for dollars, after being shipped to the United States.

Suddenly in 2020, the Fortune 500 discovered problems with their business model. During the covid epidemic, products coming from Asia simply weren't available. China, and much of the world, responded to the covid pandemic by ordering its workers to stay home.

The work stoppages of early 2020 were fairly significant, showing that the United States cannot rely on foreign production for important goods. On March 24, 2020, India ordered its entire population of 1.3 billion people to stay at home. This quarantine was the largest of the pandemic. In Argentina, the city of Buenos Aires, ordered its population to stay home for 234 days in 2020, making it the longest continuous lockdown.

China engaged in the same lockdown policies. Early in 2020, China's leader, Xi Jinping, adopted a zero covid policy. If a Chinese city had a handful of covid cases, China quarantined the entire city, until the situation improved.

During the summer of 2022, China ordered the entire city of Shanghai to stay at home. The lockdown lasted for seventy days, and created havoc in China. Many of the residents of Shanghai had difficulty getting food, because they literally could not go outside.

These shutdowns greatly interfered with China's ability to produce, and export products that the United States now deemed essential.

Empty arsenals.

America's lack of productive capacity is also affecting national defense.

In February 2022, Russia invaded Ukraine. Russia did so after the United States and Western Europe had ignored years of Russian requests to keep central Europe politically neutral.

The United States responded by rushing arms to Ukraine. Since 2022, the United States has sent more than $60 billion of weapons and economic assistance to the eastern European country. These arms shipments have demonstrated severe problems with America's defense supply chain.

One of the first problems to become evident was howitzer shells. The early years of the war in Ukraine were fought similar to the First World War. During that war, armies were bogged down in trench warfare. Each side lobbed millions of howitzer shells at the other side, hoping to gain an advantage. The same has occurred in Ukraine.

In 2022, it became apparent that the United States no longer had an industrial base capable of manufacturing large numbers of howitzer shells. When the war started, the United States had the ability to make

20,000 artillery shells per month. This was far less than the Ukraine war required.

American production was constrained for several reasons. Many of America's steel mills – formerly located in Pittsburgh; Bethlehem, Pennsylvania; and Sparrows Point, Maryland – were closed.

In addition, the United States no longer had the machine tools necessary to quickly set up weapons factories. At one key metal-making facility, 83 pieces of equipment used to make the 155mm howitzer shell were more than 50 years old. The machines were from the Vietnam war era, and had never been modernized.

In addition, the United States had difficulty sourcing raw materials. According to one government report, the Pentagon was dependent upon Russia, China and India for at least a dozen chemicals necessary to produce weapons.

For example, a howitzer shell requires trinitrotoluene, better known as TNT, for its explosive effect. No facility in the United States has made TNT since 1986. The army was dependent upon imports, for TNT. Our nation's first military leader, George Washington, would not have been pleased.

Ironically, the Pentagon's plan was to purchase TNT from a factory in Ukraine. However, Russia had already seized that factory, earlier in the war.

After the loss of the Ukrainian factory, the United States became dependent upon a single source of TNT, located in western Poland. The world's remaining production of the chemical was in China and India. Both countries were reluctant to export TNT to the United States, for fear of offending Russia.

The United States also lacked a second critical component for making howitzer shells – gun powder. Gone are the days, when John Wayne could say, "You better believe it mister, or you're dead where you stand." Today, the United States can barely make the bullets necessary to back up that threat.

Gun powder is different from TNT. As noted above, TNT creates a weapon's explosive force. Gun powder launches the shell, when it is fired from the howitzer. It is the propellant that gets the shell to enemy lines. Ukraine required a lot of gun powder. Typically, shells would be fired about fifteen miles to the front line.

In 2022, the U.S. Army's sole gunpowder plant was located in rural Virginia. It opened in 1941. At the beginning of the Ukraine War, the plant was hopelessly out of date. Modernizations were expected. In 2012, the Army signed a deal to replace the plant with a modern, more efficient plant. However, as of 2022, the replacement plant was a decade behind schedule. Thus, the United States was having difficulty obtaining gun powder.

In addition to supply problems, the United States couldn't get quality right, for making 155 mm howitzer shells. Manufacturing defects repeatedly caused production-line shutdowns early in the war. At one point, cracks in the metal shells reduced production by 50%, for months.

Rather than manufacture the metal shells, the Pentagon decided to rely upon more imports. In 2022, the United States bought 100,000 artillery shells from South Korea. The Koreans were reluctant to give the United States more shells, given their own need to maintain military readiness against North Korea.

The United States turned to Australia, for assistance in making the shells. The United States gave the Australians technical data on how to build 155 mm howitzer shells, and entered into a contract for supply.

Australia is currently building a facility to manufacture the shells. The facility is expected to produce 15,000 rounds annually by 2028, with the potential to scale up to 100,000 rounds per year. It will take some time to get Australian production online.

Meanwhile, the United States continued to approach South Korea to solve the problem. In April 2023, the Pentagon entered into an agreement with South Korea to "borrow" 500,000 artillery shells from South Korea. According to a Korean newspaper, the deal is intended to give Washington "greater flexibility" in supplying Ukraine with artillery shells.

However, artillery shells are just the tip of the pyramid. America's entire defense industrial base has collapsed, along with America's manufacturing economy.

In 2013, the Alliance for American Manufacturing found that the United States was dependent on foreign nations to produce a wide array of defense-related items, including fighter jets, steel armor plate for tanks, night vision goggles, and lithium ion batteries.

A more recent report from Govini, a commercial data company, has found that many items required for national defense are no longer made in any of the fifty states. According to Govini "just 25 well-constructed attacks . . . could cripple much of America's manufacturing apparatus for producing advanced weapons."

According to the Govini study, "more than 40% of the semiconductors that sustain American weapons systems depend on Chinese suppliers." Of particular concern, Chinese semiconductor suppliers are inextricably linked to vital weapons systems, such as the B-2 Bomber and the Patriot air-defense missile.

According to one senior official, the defense industrial base has shrunk by more than 40% in the last ten years. During his first term in office, President Donald Trump asked the government to prepare a report on the status of the defense industrial base. Trump's order directed the Secretary of Defense to assess the situation, and propose recommendations.

In 2018, the Department of Defense reported its findings. The report found that the defense industrial base was shrinking because the United States was losing critical markets for its products, and critical suppliers for raw materials. In most cases, China had taken these markets from the United States, and was now producing goods in lieu of the United States.

The report found a "surprising level of dependence" on "foreign competitor nations." More significantly, the report found that "many sectors continue to move critical capabilities offshore in pursuit of competitive pricing."

According to the report, between 2000 and 2010, over two-thirds of U.S. manufacturing saw production declines. In those same years, the United States lost over 66,000 manufacturing facilities. Many defense-related companies closed entirely. As a result, today the Pentagon relies upon foreign supply chains for a wide array of items.

The report summarized its conclusions as follows: "As America's industrial base has weakened, so too have critical workforce skills ranging from industrial welding, to high-technology skills for cybersecurity and aerospace." A lack of skilled manufacturing workers is "destabilizing workforce readiness and leading to skill atrophy."

The report found China's dominance of rare earth minerals particularly troubling. According to the report, "China has flooded the global market with rare earth minerals at subsidized prices, driven out competitors, and deterred new market entrants." As a result, the United States and its allies produce a small percentage of the world's requirements for these minerals. The Pentagon report expressed concern that China could embargo rare earth minerals.

The Pentagon report also expressed concern about American reliance on Chinese-made electronics. Since 2000, United States production of circuit boards has declined by 70%. Today, Asia accounts for 90% of world production of circuit boards, with China producing half of that amount. As of 2017, only one of the top twenty circuit board manufacturers was based in the United States. The report raised the concern that China could create "Trojan" chips, that could be remotely turned off, in the event of a conflict. China could also include viruses in computer software used to operate its electronics.

The report mentioned the decline in America's machine tool industry. The United States once led the world, in the production and export of high-end machine tools. However, since 2015, China has taken over this role. In that year, China was the world's number one exporter of machine tools.

As of 2015, China produced nearly $25 billion dollars of machine tools, or about 28% of global production. In comparison, the United States produced less than one sixth of this number – only $4.6 billion of machine tools. United States production ranked fifth in the world, after China, Japan, Germany, Italy and South Korea.

The report found that China was the sole supplier for a number of specialty chemicals used in munitions and missiles. There was no other known source for these materials. According to the report, "a sudden and catastrophic loss of supply would disrupt DoD missile, satellite, space launch, and other defense manufacturing programs. In many cases, there are no substitutes readily available."

As explained below, America's inability to produce extends to the nation's shipyards. Gone are the days, when the United States could put an armada of 1,000 ships on the shores of France.

Empty shipyards.

In 1951, the United States launched a luxury liner called the USS United States. The ship has three red and white smokestacks, that made it look somewhat like the fabled Titanic. The Titanic, built 40 years earlier, was 100 feet smaller than the United States. At 990 feet long, the USS United States was five city blocks long. On its maiden voyage, the United States broke the speed record across the Atlantic, in both directions.

The United States was decommissioned in 1969, due to the growth of air travel. Between 1996 and 2025, the ship sat rusting at a dock on the Delaware River, in Philadelphia. In 2025, the ship was moved to Mobile, Alabama, where it will be sunk and used as an artificial reef for divers. The sinking of the ship is a good metaphor for the state of America's shipyards.

During World War II, America's shipyards employed over a million people. These shipyards built literally thousands of ships during the war. This included 110 aircraft carriers of various types. The United

States also built over 150 floating dry docks, which were used for ship repair at forward bases.

The famous D-Day invasion of Europe would not have been possible without American shipbuilding capacity. On the morning of the invasion, the Germans guarding the French beaches were astonished to see over one thousand ships off the coast, that were not present the previous evening. Those ships were largely built in the United States, in record time during the war.

At the end of the Second World War, the U.S. Navy operated a dozen shipyards, servicing 10,000 ships. In addition, the United States had approximately twenty private shipyards, making ships for the world.

Those days are now long gone. As of 2025, more than half of our World War II shipyards are closed and rusting.

According to the U.S. Congressional Research Service, our nation builds only about 5 ocean-going vessels a year. In comparison, China builds about a 1,000 such ships every year. That's a difference of 200 to 1, in favor of China.

In terms of tonnage, the United States produces about 100,000 tons of ships every year. That sounds like a lot, until we realize that China produces more than 23 million tons of ships each year. That's a difference of 230 to 1, in favor of China. That means that the United States is producing less than 1% of the ships that China produces.

The U.S. Navy has confirmed these numbers. According to a slide leaked from the Pentagon, China's shipbuilding capacity is 232 times greater than that of the United States. Thus, in a conflict between the United States and China, China could build more than 200 ships for every vessel made in the United States.

So what happened? Why was America's shipbuilding industry wiped out?

The answer is cost. No one wants to buy a ship made in the United States because the cost is too high. China, South Korea, and Japan build ships much more cheaply than the United States.

Since there is no demand for American-made ships, our nation's industrial base for shipbuilding has withered. Shipbuilding requires the ability to manufacture steel plate, propellers, and engines. Increasingly, the United States does not produce these things.

Nikkei Asia – a Japanese newspaper – recently interviewed the president of a large Japanese shipbuilding company, concerning American supply chains for making ships. The executive, Yukito Higaki, says that it is nearly impossible to build a ship in the United States today. The United States doesn't have the industrial base to do so.

Higaki says that his company would have to import nearly 200,000 components from Japan to the United States, to assemble a single ship. He says that this is not cost-effective. "Bringing parts to a place where there's no supply chain is . . . difficult," says Higaki. He estimates that it would take between five and ten years to establish a supplier network in the United States.

Our nation's lack of industrial capacity is starting to affect military preparedness. China recently overtook the United States in terms of the size of its navy. China now has about 350 "battle force" ships, compared to 300 ships for the United States.

Despite the smaller size, the U.S. Navy can't even maintain the ships that it has. The Navy recently started maintaining its vessels in Japan and South Korea, due to lack of capacity in the United States.

In other words, our nation has grown so weak that we can't even maintain our own navy, without relying upon the assistance of a former adversary. The World War II generation – which fought Japan – must be rolling over in its grave.

Empty textile mills.

During the Second World War, the United States provided billions of dollars of aid to the Soviet Union, to help with its fight against the Nazis.

The numbers are astonishing, even today. The United States sent Russia 400,000 vehicles, 14,000 aircraft, 13,000 tanks, 8,000 tractors, 4.5 million tons of food, 107,000 tons of cotton, and 2.7 million tons of petroleum products, as well as millions of blankets, uniforms, and boots.

This materiel was essential for winning the war. If you read the memoirs of German soldiers who fought on the eastern front during the war, they talk about being chased out of Russia by American-made trucks. In comparison, the German armies were starving, and were forced to walk out of Eastern Europe.

It is unlikely that the United States could replicate this achievement today.

For example, let's consider whether the United States has the ability to mass produce uniforms and boots, in the event of a war. The answer is likely no.

In 2024, the United States was dependent upon imported goods, to cover its clothing and shoe needs. In that year, the United States imported 2.1 billion pairs of shoes. That is about six pairs of shoes for every person in the United States.

Not surprisingly, the United States is dependent upon China for most of these imports. Nearly 60% of America's imported shoes – about 1.2 billion pairs of shoes – came from China. The remaining 880 million pairs came from elsewhere on the planet.

In 2024, the United States manufactured a paltry 25 million pairs of shoes. That is less than one pair of shoes for every ten people in the United States. If the United States had to manufacture its own shoes, Americans would be forced to wear used shoes – or none at all – for several years, until we could import tools to start making shoes again.

American domestic shoe production pales in comparison to Chinese shoe production. China makes more than 50 times the shoes made by the United States. And that number is just the shoes destined for the USA. China also produces billions of pairs of shoes for its own population, and for elsewhere on the planet.

What a change! In 1945, the United States provided millions of pairs of army boots to Russia. And now – eighty years later – the United States can barely make shoes for its own population. How did we get here?

The answer is government protection. Prior to 1945, the United States protected its textile industry. After 1945, the United States dismantled the industry, and relied on imported goods. Let's take a look at the history.

During the Industrial Revolution, Britain learned to mass produce cloth by means of steam powered machinery. Prior to 1800, the United States did not have this technology. The United States relied upon imported cloth from Britain.

In the early 1800s, the United States imposed tariffs on British fabrics. The tariffs created an incentive to produce cloth in the United States. Within a few years, the United States learned the secrets of Britain's textile mills, and began to produce its own cloth. Throughout the 19th century, America's textile business grew stronger.

In the 1930s, Japan began to threaten American textile production. The United States responded by imposing restrictions on cloth imported from Japan. These restrictions had the effect of increasing the price of clothing in the United States. By 1960, the typical American family spent about 10% of family income on clothing and shoes. This was equivalent to about $5,000 today.

However, that 10% payment came with certain security. The clothes were all made in the United States. The United States had the ability to grow its own cotton, weave the cotton into cloth, and manufacture its own clothing.

The United States continued to protect its markets for another generation. In 1962, the United States entered into a "voluntary restraint agreement" with Japan, regarding textiles. The agreement restricted the amount of clothing that Japan could export to America.

Voluntary restraint agreements – known as VRAs – became a central feature of United States policy regarding the textile industry. In the 1950s, the United States applied VRAs to other Asian producers, including Hong Kong, India, and Taiwan. The agreements established quotas, which allowed these countries to export a certain amount of textile products to the United States. By 1972, the United States had entered into VRAs with thirty different countries. That number increased to forty countries, by 1994.

Nevertheless, American production of clothing began to drop. By the early 1980s, American production of clothing had fallen to about 70% of domestic consumption.

In 1995, the Clinton administration decided to phase out the import restrictions. As the restraint agreements expired, American textile jobs disappeared. Between 1990 and 2011, about 750,000 apparel manufacturing jobs in the United States went overseas. Today, only about 85,000 garment workers remain in the United States. That is nearly a 90% drop.

Today, American clothing companies order virtually all of their clothes from overseas. For example, in 2003, Gap, a clothing retailer, sourced its inventory from more than 1,200 different factories in more than forty countries.

Meanwhile, the United States continues to lose textile jobs. In just six months during 2023, eight textile manufacturers closed factories in the United States:

- Hanes Brands closed its hosiery plant in Clarksville, Arkansas, and laid off 330 workers. The plant was the last Hanes facility in the United States.
- Gildan closed a textile plant in Salisbury, North Carolina, with 250 jobs lost.
- Milliken closed two plants in South Carolina, and one in North Carolina.
- Parkdale Mills, a yarn company, closed three plants in Hillsville, Virginia, and a facility in Graniteville, South Carolina. Over 300 employees were laid off.
- National Spinning shut the doors at its last yarn-spinning facility in Whiteville, North Carolina. One hundred employees lost their jobs.

As American factories have closed, America's imports of clothing have dramatically increased. In 2024, the United States imported $107 billion of textiles and apparel, primarily from China, Vietnam and India.

Today, it is estimated that the United States produces only about 2.5% of the clothing that it uses. Steve Lamar, the president of the American Apparel and Footwear Association, recently said that the United States does not "have the labor, skill set, materials, and infrastructure" to manufacture clothing and shoes on a large scale.

Thus, in the event of a war, it is unlikely that the United States would have the ability to outfit a large army, or to provide for the clothing needs of the population.

My kingdom for a computer chip.

In recent years, the United States has faced a critical inability to acquire computer chips.

In November 2022, Ford's CEO, Jim Farley, told the media that his company was having difficulty getting enough computer chips to make cars. Farley said that Ford's North American employees had worked a full week only three times in 2022, because of a chip shortage. According to Farley, Ford could not produce 40,000 vehicles because it couldn't get a chip that usually cost just forty cents.

As with ventilators, America could not produce silicon chips. These problems were the result of years of outsourcing America's computer chip production.

The United States invented the transistor at Bell Labs in 1947. During the 1950s, the United States placed more and more transistors on a single piece of silicon, creating the silicon chip. By the 1960s, the United States dominated world production of computer chips.

However, after 1970, the United States began to outsource production of computer chips to Asia, initially to Japan. Later, the United States helped set up chipmaking industries in Taiwan and South Korea. American chip production suffered, as a result. By the early 1990s, the United States only produced 37% of the world's supply of computer chips.

In 1992, a group of computer manufacturers asked the United States government to subsidize computer chip manufacturing in the United States.

The Clinton administration was not enthusiastic about the request. According to Clinton's economists, it didn't matter whether the United States manufactured chips in the United States, or overseas. A reporter asked Michael Boskin, the Chairman of the White House Council of Economic Advisors, if the United States should subsize the production of computer chips. Boskin allegedly replied, "Potato chips, computer chips . . . what's the difference?"

Boskin's statement was widely criticized at the time, and Boskin later denied making the comment. However, the comment reflected the thinking of many economists at the time. In the early 1990s, America's economists didn't care whether the United States had a computer chip industry. They were proponents of free trade, which said that it didn't matter what goods were bought or sold.

As of 2022, the United States manufactured only about 12% of the computer chips produced in the world. Even worse, the United States had no ability to produce the world's fastest chips, made with cutting-edge technologies. This meant that the United States did not have the ability to produce chips for its advanced fighter jet, the F35.

The United States also does not have the ability to produce machines capable of manufacturing the smallest, fastest, and most advanced chips. This technology is known as extreme ultraviolet (EUV) lithography. In the 1990s, American scientists at Sandia National Laboratory and

Lawrence Livermore helped develop EUV technology. However, the United States did not fully capitalize on the technology.

Instead, the Dutch did so. The Dutch company, Advanced Semiconductor Materials Lithography (ASML), is the only company in the world that can build an entire EUV lithography machine. These machines, the size of a double-decker bus, contain more than 10,000 components and weigh 180 tons. America lost out on the production of this valuable product, in part, because the Clinton administration did not see an advantage in manufacturing in the United States.

As of 2025, Taiwan dominates world production of computer chips. Taiwan imports these huge lithography machines from Holland, and then uses the machines to make chips for the world's companies. Taiwan's leading company, Taiwan Semiconductor Manufacturing Company (TSMC), manufactures 68% of the world's chips. More importantly, TSMC makes over 90% of the world's most advanced chips.

Taiwan's dominance of the chip market poses a problem for Pentagon. This is because Taiwan could potentially be under Chinese control, by the end of the decade. As you may recall, Taiwan is engaged in a civil war with the People's Republic of China. Mainland China is intent on defeating the government of Taiwan, and bringing Taipei under its control.

When the United States exported its chip production to Taiwan in the 1980s, the Pentagon assumed that the United States would always be capable of defending Taiwan from China, and ensuring that the chip factories would remain under United States control. That critical assumption changed in August 2022.

On August 2, 2022, Nancy Pelosi, the Speaker of the U.S. House of Representatives visited Taiwan, to show support for the Taiwanese government. The People's Republic of China responded to Pelosi's visit by conducting live-fire exercises in the vicinity of Taiwan. For the next ten days, the Chinese navy encircled Taiwan, and shut down flights in and out of Taiwan. The exercises made it clear that already China has sufficient military power to take control of the island, together with Taiwan's microchip factories.

The United States responded to China's show of force by seeking to set up a domestic source of computer chips. On August 9, 2022 – just days after Pelosi's visit to Taiwan – Congress enacted the CHIPS and Science Act. The Act provides $52.7 billion for American semiconductor research, development, and manufacturing. This includes $39 billion in manufacturing incentives, to produce silicon chips in the United States.

Since 2022, the United States has been engaged in an emergency effort to set up the world's most advanced computer chip factories in the United States. During this time, the U.S. government has pressured Taiwan's largest chipmaking company – TSMC – to set up production in the United States.

TSMC has agreed to work with the United States. In just three years, TSMC has set up an advanced chipmaking facility – known as a "fab" – in Arizona. TSMC is now building two, more advanced fabs in Arizona. Altogether, TSMC has agreed to invest an astonishing $165 billion in the United States.

However, other companies are facing delays in making chips in the United States. Korea's largest chip manufacturer, Samsung, is building a fab in Texas. However, as of 2025, Samsung has delayed construction of the factory, due to a lack of customers. Intel is also facing delays. Intel's new fab in Ohio is not scheduled to be operational until the early 2030s, due to supply chain issues and a lack of qualified employees.

Thus, as of 2025, the United States has belatedly addressed its supply chain vulnerabilities, involving computer chips. However, the United States is not out of the woods yet. Meanwhile, our nation is falling behind in other areas as well – namely the race to dominate space.

Falling behind in the space race.

There is evidence that our nation's inability to manufacture is affecting national security in other ways. We are falling behind China in the race to control space.

In 2017, President Trump directed America's space agency, NASA, to send a new crewed mission to the moon. To do so, NASA has had to overcome several large hurdles.

In 2017, the United States had not launched a crewed mission to space in more than six years. This was due to the disaster involving the space shuttle Columbia, in 2003. After the Columbia disaster, NASA considered the shuttle too risky to fly. As a result, NASA cancelled the space shuttle program. After 2011, the United States relied upon Russian rockets to send astronauts to the International Space Station.

To get to the moon, the United States first needed a rocket capable of getting to the Space Station. NASA asked Boeing and Space X to do the job. Space X was the first to solve the problem. On May 30, 2020, Space X successfully launched astronauts to the space station. However, after nearly ten years, Boeing has not successfully done so.

On June 5, 2024, Boeing launched two astronauts to the International Space Station. Before reaching the station, Boeing's Starliner spacecraft developed helium leaks. The leaks interfered with the jets necessary to control the Starliner in space. Fortunately, the spacecraft was able to successfully dock with the space station.

However, Boeing was not able to get the astronauts back to earth. The two astronauts, Sunita Williams and Butch Wilmore, were forced to remain on the space station for over nine months, until SpaceX was able to send a spacecraft to retrieve them.

NASA has also had difficulty putting an unmanned lander on the moon.

On January 8, 2024, a private U.S. company launched a Vulcan Centaur rocket from Cape Canaveral, on a mission to the moon. The rocket developed a propellant leak shortly after launch. As a result, the spacecraft never left Earth orbit. The spacecraft re-entered the atmosphere ten days later, on January 18, 2024, and burned up on re-entry.

On February 9, 2024, a second private company – Intuitive Machines – tried a second time to put a lander on the moon. The spacecraft reached the south pole of the moon. However, the spacecraft came in too fast, skidded and fell over. One of the lander's six legs was broken. The lander ceased to function shortly thereafter.

The United States finally put a lander on the moon on March 2, 2025. On that day, a private company known as Firefly Aerospace, successfully placed a lander on the moon. As of early March 2025, the lander – known as the Blue Ghost – remained operational. This was the first American spacecraft to land on the moon in more than fifty years, since the final Apollo mission in 1972.

NASA is also having difficulty building the gigantic rocket necessary to get the astronauts to the moon.

One would think that NASA would be an expert at this sort of thing. Between 1968 and 1972, the United States flew ten crewed missions to the moon. The Apollo moon program took 24 American astronauts from Earth to the moon. Of these astronauts, twelve actually walked on the surface of the moon. All of the astronauts returned home safely.

The Apollo program relied upon a rocket known as the Saturn V. The Saturn V was the largest and most powerful rocket ever built. The first stage of the rocket consisted of five jet engines, each generating over 1.5 million pounds of thrust. It consisted of three million parts, and was taller than the Statue of Liberty.

NASA has asked Elon Musk's company, Space X, to replicate the Saturn V rocket, for purposes of the new moon program. In interviews, Musk has suggested that the United States has lost some technology necessary to go to the moon.

SpaceX has found that many of the designs for the Saturn V rocket no longer exist. The blueprints were created by hundreds of engineering firms, and in many cases, had not been preserved. NASA literally had to go to a museum, and study the Saturn V rocket, to try figure out how the machine was built.

There is an appearance that SpaceX is trying to recreate the wheel, in the new Artemis moon program. As of June 2025, at least nine of Space X's rockets have blown up, in various stages of the testing process.

On paper, the United States is aiming to put astronauts back on the moon in 2027. However, it is questionable as to whether the United States will be ready by that date. The United States faces a major technological hurdle. NASA's lunar lander – a modified SpaceX Starship – will require in-orbit refueling. That has never been done before.

In February 2025, Dan Dumbacher, a former senior Nasa official, told Congress that "the probability of the United States safely landing humans on the moon by 2030, with the current plan, is remote at best."

Meanwhile, China is moving forward rapidly with its own plans for human exploration of the moon. Over the past fifteen years, China has landed numerous spacecraft on the moon.

In 2010, China's Chang'e 2 spacecraft orbited and mapped the moon.

In December 2013, China successfully placed a lander and rover on the moon, in its Chang'e 3 mission. This was the first time in four decades that a country had accomplished a soft landing on the moon.

In May 2018, China became the first country in the world to place a satellite in orbit on the far side of the moon. The satellite, Queqiao-1, does not orbit the moon. Instead, the satellite orbits a point of equilibrium – known as L2 – that is located beyond both the Earth and the moon. In that position, the Queqiao-1 satellite is able to provide constant communication between Earth and the far side of the moon. As of 2025, the United States has no similar capability.

In December 2018, China successfully landed a spacecraft on the far side of the moon, in its Chang'e 4 mission. This was the first time that any nation had landed on the dark side of the moon, which always faces away from the Earth.

In 2020, China successfully collected rocks from the moon, and returned them to earth. In 2024, China collected rocks from the far side of the moon, in its Chang'e 6 mission, and returned them to earth.

China plans to land two astronauts on the moon prior to 2030. China is preparing a rocket for the mission. The Long March-10 rocket could make its maiden flight as early as 2026.

China has already started planning for a permanent base on the moon. It intends to complete the base by 2035. China is testing a process for making bricks from lunar soil. In 2028, during an unmanned mission to the moon, China intends to test the brickmaking process on the moon.

Thus, as of 2025, China is decisively ahead of the United States in space technology. While the United States is trying to reverse engineer the achievements of its engineers from fifty years ago, China is moving forward with success after success.

Rare earth minerals – China's grip on the U.S.

Rare earth elements are 17 little-known minerals, which are essential for modern manufacturing. They are used to produce solar panels, car batteries, powerful magnets, silicon chips, and other high-tech products.

Rare earth elements are of critical importance for our nation's defense. For example, an F35 fighter jet requires 935 pounds of rare earth elements. A Virginia-class submarine requires over 10,000 pounds of rare earth minerals, in its manufacture. They are used in the submarine's Tomahawk missiles, radar, and drive motors.

The United States played a significant role in the development of rare earth elements. In the 1940s, the United States learned how to separate and purify these minerals. This was necessary for the development of the first atomic bomb, in the Manhattan Project.

After the war, the United States led the world in the production of rare earth elements. In 1974, the United States accounted for 78% of global production of these minerals.

In the 1970s and 1980s, China's President, Deng Xiaoping, designated rare earth minerals as a strategic resource. China began to pour resources into the industry. As Japan did a century earlier, China brought in foreign experts to learn how to process rare earth minerals. "The Middle East has oil, China has rare earths," Deng said.

In the 1990s, Chinese production of rare earth elements began to undercut American production, in terms of price.

The United States began to cede market share to the Chinese. It was easier to produce rare earth minerals in China than the United States, due to China's then-lack of environmental laws. Refining rare earth minerals can release heavy metals, acids, and radioactive materials into the environment. This poses a threat to water supplies. Mining also produces large amounts of dust.

By 2017, the United States produced no rare earth minerals. Virtually no one in the United States, other than a few people at the Pentagon, cared about the lack of U.S. production. Chinese-produced rare earth minerals were cheap, and readily available. No one remembered that Deng Xiaoping planned to use the minerals to gain a chokehold on world production.

Today, China controls most of the world's supply chain for rare earth minerals. A large portion of these elements are mined in China. China then performs 89% of the separation work, and 90% of the refining of these elements. Once the elements are refined, they are made into high tech products, such as high-powered magnets. China controls 92% of the global market for these specialized magnets.

In the early 2020s, American leaders began to realize that the United States was vulnerable to Chinese pressure, involving rare earth elements. In 2023, the United States reopened a single mine, to obtain these elements. The United States now supplies 14% of world output. However, our nation does not have the ability to process these minerals.

Most of American production is first sent to China, and then processed there.

China's control of rare earth minerals directly threatens our nation's security.

In December 2024, China banned the export of gallium, germanium, and antimony to the United States. These minerals are used in semiconductors, military equipment, and other industrial applications. China also banned the export of superhard minerals to the United States. These bans have affected our nation's ability to produce weapons.

In early 2025, China announced that it would require licenses for the export of rare earth minerals to other countries, including the United States. China wanted to restrict the export of these elements, if the minerals could be used by foreign militaries.

After China's announcement of the license requirement, China's exports of rare-earth magnets to the United States fell overnight. In May 2025, China's exports of rare earth magnets to the United States fell 93%, from a year earlier. Prices for rare earth minerals tripled overnight.

All countries were affected by the new licensing requirement. Shipments of rare earth magnets to Germany in April and May 2025 fell by 55%, compared to 2024. Shipments to South Korea were down 81%.

Within weeks, car manufacturers worldwide announced that they were on the verge of closing factories, due to the lack of rare earth minerals. In May 2025, Suzuki Motor suspended production of cars at a plant in Japan, because it could not get enough rare earth magnets. That same month, Ford Motor Company stopped production at a factory in Chicago. Lisa Drake, a vice-president overseeing Ford's supply chain, said "It's hand to mouth," in terms of Ford's supply of magnets.

AMERICA HAS VOLUNTARILY DISARMED

President Trump was forced to make significant concessions to China, to get the rare earth elements flowing again. To placate China, Trump reduced tariffs on Chinese goods from 150%, to about 40%. When the Chinese continued dragging their feet on approving export licenses, Trump was forced to lift curbs on computer chip design tools, badly sought-after by China. Trump also allowed chipmakers, such as Nvidia, to resume selling artificial intelligence chips to China.

Experts estimate that it will take the United States years to replicate China's supply chain for rare earth elements.

America's import reliance on critical materials.

Rare earth minerals are just the tip of the iceberg. The United States also relies on imports for a wide variety of critical materials.

For example, as of 2025, the United States has no cobalt mine, and no refinery -- even though we have plenty of cobalt in Minnesota, Alaska, Michigan and Missouri. We are dependent upon foreign supplies for this critical mineral.

The United States has one nickel mine. However, we do not have the ability to process the material. We send our domestic nickel to Canada and other overseas smelters for processing.

We have a similar situation with copper. We have several copper mines, but only two copper smelters. As a result, the United States sends nearly half of its copper overseas for processing.

The Trump administration has recently established a critical minerals list. There are 50 minerals on the last. Of these, the United States imports the majority of our supply for 43 minerals. Our dependence on foreign production is astonishing. Below is a sample from the list:

Table 2.1

United States Mineral Reliance

Mineral	Net Import Reliance	Primary Supplier
Arsenic	100%	China
Fluorspar	100%	Mexico
Gallium	100%	China
Graphite	100%	China
Indium	100%	Republic of Korea
Manganese	100%	Gabon
Rare earths	95%	China
Titanium	95%	Japan
Chromium	83%	South Africa
Tin	77%	Peru
Cobalt	76%	Norway
Zinc	76%	Canada
Aluminum	75%	Jamaica
Platinum	66%	South Africa
Germanium	50%	China

China is our primary supplier for many of these materials. For example, the United States imports 100% of its gallium, and 50% of its germanium, primarily from China. This is a critical bottleneck.

Gallium and germanium are used in the production of transistors, semiconductors, solar panels, LED lights and fiber optic systems.

In August 2023, China announced export restrictions on gallium and germanium, as part of the trade war between our countries. China's restrictions are another reminder that it is China – and not the United States – that dominates the world's supply chains today.

America's food vulnerability.

If you drive along the border between the United States and Mexico, in McAllen, Texas, you will see large refrigerated warehouses on the United States side. These warehouses are filled with fruit, vegetables and meat, imported from Mexico and Central America.

These warehouses are a symbol of America's vulnerability in the production of food.

For many years, the United States ran a trade surplus in the production of food. Until recently, we earned a surplus of about $30 billion a year, from the export of corn, wheat, soybeans, chickens, hogs, and cattle.

However, that surplus is a thing of the past. Like our factories, our food production system has become hollowed out. In 2019, the United States began to run a trade deficit in food products. That deficit has continued to grow each year. The U.S. Department of Agriculture expects the deficit to reach over $50 billion in 2025.

Today, the United States is dependent upon a wide variety of imported food.

Some of the products are obvious – such as bananas. Each year, the United States imports over five million tons of bananas. We import a lot of avocados, too – over a million tons a year – primarily from Mexico, Peru and Columbia.

However, increasingly, we are running a deficit in all types of food, other than grains.

In 2024, the United States imported over four billion pounds of beef, primarily from Mexico, Argentina, Australia and Brazil. This was an increase of nearly 25% from the prior year. According to Wells Fargo, imported beef now accounts for about 8% of U.S. beef consumption. All of this imported beef is putting pressure on U.S. suppliers. Margins are razor thin, causing some American companies to go out of business. The size of the U.S. cattle herd is at the lowest level in 74 years, according to the American Farm Bureau Federation.

The cost of this imported beef adds up. Each year, the United States has a deficit of nearly $11 billion, for imported meat and seafood. This deficit should be a warning sign to the American people. It means that the United States is not shipping goods to Mexico, Brazil and Australia to pay for this imported beef. We are paying for these hamburgers, with printed dollars, which these countries may not accept in the future.

In the event of a balance of payments crisis, the United States may have difficulty putting beef on the bun, at your local McDonalds. Other parts of your hamburger will likely be missing as well. For example, consider lettuce. Surprisingly, our nation is not self-sufficient in the production of lettuce. In 2023, the United States imported half a billion dollars of lettuce, primarily from Mexico and Canada.

Your hamburger may also be missing tomatoes, in the event of a currency crisis. Given the current value of the dollar, it is cheaper for the United States to import tomatoes, rather than grow them locally. In 2023, the United States imported nearly $3 billion of tomatoes. That was nearly two-thirds of the greenhouse-grown tomatoes consumed in the United States that year. We are also running a large deficit for general food products, beverages and tobacco.

How things have changed since World War II!

In the 1940s, the United States was self-sufficient in food production. This enabled the United States to export large amounts of food to support the war effort. Between 1940 and 1945, the United States exported 4.5 million tons of food to England and Russia each. This included approximately 130 million cans of Spam.

It is unlikely that the United States could replicate these achievements today. As of 2025, the United States has a trade surplus only in the production of grains, such as corn and wheat. We, as a nation, are otherwise dependent upon food from outside of our borders.

America's dependence on imported food raises a question as to whether the United States has an adequate food security. The United States is able to import this extravaganza of food because the world is willing to accept printed dollars. If the world were to reject the U.S. dollar – and insist on a different unit of trade – then the United States would likely not be able to import its existing supply of food. This is a real concern that policymakers need to address.

The U.S. economy is hollowed out.

If you drive from coast to coast in the United States, you could easily get the impression that the United States is a gigantic playground. You will see a lot of gas stations, fast food restaurants, and shopping malls. You wouldn't be wrong. Since 1950, the United States has developed an economy that prioritizes consumption. Our nation has 160,000 gas stations, and nearly a quarter million fast food restaurants. This includes 17,000 Starbucks and 13,000 McDonalds. In fact, the United States has one fast food restaurant for every 2,000 people. We have over 115,000 shopping centers. This includes both malls, and open-air plazas.

These buildings reflect the fact that our economy is seventy percent consumption.

We see this in the list of the largest employers in the United States. The twenty largest employers in America are as follows:

Table 2.2

United States First 20 Largest Employers

Rank	Company	Number of Employees
1.	Walmart Inc.	2,100,000
2.	Amazon	1,556,000
3.	Federal Express	529,000
4.	Concentrix Corporation	450,000
5.	Target Corporation	440,000
6.	Marriott International, Inc.	418,000
7.	UnitedHealth Group	400,000
8.	TriNet Group, Inc.	364,300
9.	Starbucks Corporation	361,000
10.	Cognizant Technology	336,800
11.	PepsiCo, Inc.	319,000
12.	JPMorgan Chase & Co.	317,233
13.	HCA Healthcare	316,000
14.	Insperity, Inc.	311,761
15.	Albertsons Companies	285,000
16.	IBM	270,300
17.	Aramark	266,680
18.	Microsoft Corporation	228,000
19.	Dollar Tree	214,710
20.	Walt Disney Company	214,360

AMERICA HAS VOLUNTARILY DISARMED

The above list is telling. The top three companies on the list all help our nation consume the world's goods. These are Walmart, Amazon, and Federal Express. We see these names every day. That is because they are our economy.

Next time you are in Walmart, look at the labels on the products. Virtually everything in the store is imported. The same is true for Amazon. If Amazon were forced to sell only American-made products, the company would likely have little to sell.

Other companies on the list demonstrate how empty, and hollowed-out, our economy has become. Pepsi, Target, Dollar Tree and Walt Disney are on the list. These companies provide entertainment, and consumption. In the event of a war, Target, Dollar Tree and Pepsi will provide virtually no value to the United States.

Let's take a look at the names that you may not recognize. Concentrix Corp., Cognizant Technology, TriNet and Aramark are all service corporations. Concentrix provides finance, marketing and human resource services to its clients. Cognizant is an IT technology company. TriNet Group and Aramark Corporation are human resource companies.

Not a single company in the top 20 employers manufactures anything of value. We are selling imported goods to each other. We are helping each other try on clothes, imported from Asia. We are entertaining each other. We are selling Pepsi to each other. None of this creates wealth.

Is this safe? In the event of a national emergency, can we fend for ourselves?

We have already seen that we can't make ventilators, N95 masks, and howitzer shells. We don't make 98% of our clothing. We are forced to rely upon the Koreans and the Japanese to maintain our navy ships. We don't even make enough food to feed ourselves.

If the dollar were to come down – preventing us from importing – what would the United States look like? Will there be anything for sale in the malls?

In 2010, a New York resident, Mark Andol, opened a store that sells only products manufactured in the United States. Andol had difficulty finding sophisticated products to sell. He doesn't sell *any* item that is electric, or needs a battery – because he can't find any American made products. According to Andol, "we have been to the moon but we can't build a toaster."

Let's take a look at the next twenty largest employers on the list. Will they save the United States, in the event of a balance of payments crisis? According to the U.S. government, they are:

Table 2.3

United States Next 20 Largest Employers

Rank	Company	Number of Employees
21.	Darden Restaurants, Inc.	187,384
22.	Alphabet Inc.	183,323
23.	Hilton Hotels	181,000
24.	Lear Corporation	173,700

25.	Boeing	172,000
26.	Ford Motor Company	171,000
27.	Apple Inc.	164,000
28.	GXO Logistics, Inc.	152,000
29.	Flex Ltd.	148,115
30.	AT&T Inc.	140,990
31.	CBRE Group	140,000
32.	Johnson & Johnson	138,100
33.	Jabil Inc.	138,000
34.	Tyson Foods	138,000
35.	Barrett Business Services	135,727
36.	American Airlines	133,300
37.	Chipotle Mexican Grill	130,504
38.	Tesla	125,665
39.	Amphenol Corporation	125,000
40.	Thermo Fisher Scientific	125,000

As with the first 20 employers, we are looking at a lot of consumption. Alphabet – also known as Google, Chipotle and Darden Restaurants are all consumption-driven companies.

However, we are starting to see some manufacturing. Lear and Boeing make airplanes, and Ford has manufactured cars for more than a century. Tesla makes electric cars; and Thermo Fisher produces scientific instruments.

Thus, we are starting to see some production in the United States. However, we are still looking at a consumption-driven economy. This poses risks to America's standard of living. Let's take a look at how we got here, and the problems with America's economic model.

CHAPTER 3
This Ship Will Sink

You may be familiar with the film, Titanic. The motion picture dramatizes the last hours of the ship RMS Titanic, as it sank in the early morning of April 15, 1912. After the ship struck an iceberg, the crew initially told the passengers that there was nothing to worry about. The ship's owner – the White Star Line – had claimed the vessel was "unsinkable."

However, one man on the ship understood that there were problems. That man was Thomas Andrews, the chief designer of the ship. Andrews was on board to see how the vessel performed, on its maiden voyage. As the ship's designer, Andrews knew everything about the Titanic. He knew how many boilers it had. He knew the weight of the screws, and the ship's anticipated speed.

While the other passengers were unconcerned about the collision with the iceberg, Andrews was quietly urging people to get into the lifeboats. He knew that there were not enough lifeboats to accommodate all of the passengers on board. He also knew that the ship would sink, based on the damage from the iceberg.

When the captain, Edward Smith, asked Andrews if the ship would really sink, Andrews replied, "tis a mathematical certainty." These words were carefully preserved in the subsequent government inquiry. One of the passengers, 19-year-old Jack Thayer, heard Andrews say that he expected the ship to sink within an hour.

The sinking of the Titanic is the perfect analogy for the United States.

In the United States, it is commonly believed that the American economy is "unsinkable." The media constantly tells us that our capital markets are "deep and strong," and that the dollar is the world's "safe haven" in times of storm. We are constantly told that the "nation's latest economic report card . . . is good," and that the nation's economic engine is "revved up."

Many economists share this view. In 2024, the Economic Policy Institute (EPI) – a think tank – reported that "the economy today is extraordinarily strong by nearly every historical benchmark."

EPI's website cites several reasons for optimism. These include the nation's gross domestic product (GDP), job growth, growth in real wages, and the stock market. According to EPI, the nation's GDP is growing strongly. Real GDP in the United States has risen 2.9% annually since 2022. In comparison, annual growth was only 1.8% during the decade leading up to 2019.

According to EPI, job growth in the United States has been strong, and real wages are rising. According to the Institute, inflation-adjusted wages have grown rapidly, and are reaching an all-time high.

EPI also cites the stock market. The S&P 500 has grown 19% annually since 2022 – much higher than the 6% average growth between 2007 and 2019.

All of these numbers may be true. However, these numbers do not accurately reflect the state of the U.S. economy. EPI failed to mention some important information about our economy – namely, that we are drowning in debt.

GDP does not accurately describe the economy.

Economists typically look at Gross Domestic Product, or GDP, to determine the productivity of a country. In theory, GDP measures the value of the final goods and services produced in a country, in a given period of time.

The idea of GDP was first used in 1934 by economist Simon Kuznets, in a report to Congress. Later in that decade, Kuznets warned that his definition of Gross Domestic Product could be over-simplified. He wrote that GDP could "become dangerous" and mislead policymakers, if not properly defined. In other words, GDP can produce an illusion of accuracy, that is not real.

Kuznets was correct in warning policymakers of problems with GDP. The number doesn't compare "apples to apples" in comparing economies, because the number treats consumption the same as production.

If one nation spends a trillion dollars producing goods, and another nation spends a trillion dollars consuming those goods, GDP treats the two economies as the same. This is an astonishing error, that the United States does not take into account.

For example, the port of Los Angeles is the busiest container port in the Western hemisphere. In 2024, the port handled 10.3 million shipping containers, having an average length of twenty feet. A large portion of these containers were from China.

When a container, filled with shirts from China, is taken off a boat, and placed in a storage yard at the Port of Los Angeles, the U.S. Bureau of Economic Analysis considers the labor of the port workers to be part of the nation's GDP.

When a truck driver picks up the container, and hauls the shirts to a Target warehouse in St. Louis, the truck driver's salary is also included in GDP. According to the government, the truck driver has materially contributed to the nation's economy.

When Target employees unload the container, and deliver the shirts to a Target store, the Bureau of Economic Analysis includes their salary in the nation's GDP. According to the bureau, wages paid to warehouse workers are included in the calculation of the "final cost" of goods and services "produced" in the United States. Finally, when the goods are sold, the salary of the sales clerk is included in GDP.

At the end of the day, the U.S. government believes that the United States has created a huge amount of wealth – or GDP – in the transaction. In reality, the United States has simply consumed gasoline and the time of several dozen people, to consume a shipping container full of shirts.

Now, look at the transaction from the Chinese point of view. To fill that container, China most likely needed to import cotton to produce cloth. After spinning the cloth, China needed to cut the cloth, and sew it into shirts. These shirts were then carefully packaged, placed in boxes, and loaded onto the container, destined for Los Angeles.

Suppose, hypothetically, that it cost the United States $100,000 to receive the container, deliver the shirts to St. Louis, and then sell the shirts at Target. Suppose that it cost China the same amount – $100,000 – to import the cotton, manufacture the shirts, and deliver the shirts to Los Angeles.

The Bureau of Economic Analysis treats these two transactions identically. It says that U.S. GDP, in this transaction, is the same as Chinese GDP. Both nations produced $100,000 of "value" in the transaction.

The Bureau of Economic Analysis is, of course, wrong. China has produced $100,000 of value. It has produced and delivered a container filled with shirts to its customer in North America. In reality, the United States has produced no value, at all. The United States has consumed $100,000 of value, produced by China.

We are now starting to see that GDP does not accurately compare nations. The number is worthless, as currently defined. GDP is defined to be a bloated, worthless number, because the politicians that control the Bureau of Economic Analysis want us to think that the United States is being "productive" and "growing."

For example, America's leaders like to boast that the U.S. economy is the largest in the world. They cite their fictional number, GDP, as evidence. In 2024, United States GDP was supposedly $29 trillion. In comparison, Chinese GDP during the same period was $19 trillion.

This would seem to suggest that the United States economy is about 50% larger than that of China. Nothing could be further from the truth. China's economy is actually significantly larger than that of the United States.

To understand this, we have to look at different metrics, that tell the real story. For example, let's look at steel production. In 2020, China produced 1,020 million tons of steel. In comparison, in 2020, the United States produced 72.7 million metric tons of steel. In other words, China produced more than 14 times the amount of steel which the United States produced.

In the event of a war, China would literally bury the United States with bombs, bullets, drones, trucks, tanks, and aircraft carriers. We have already seen that China's shipbuilding capacity is 232 times greater than that of the United States. This is partly due to the fact that China produces 14 times more steel than the United States.

Let's take a look at aluminum production. In 2022, China produced 42 million tons of aluminum. In comparison, in 2022, the United States produced 861,000 tons of aluminum. In other words, China produced nearly 49 times the amount of aluminum produced in the United States that year.

Aluminum is used for a wide variety of products. These include cars, aircraft, windows, electrical wiring, and consumer goods. The numbers for aluminum production suggest that China's economy is vastly bigger, and stronger, than that of the United States.

Let's look at production of motor vehicles. China is the world's largest producer of cars and trucks. In 2024, China produced over 30 million vehicles. This represents more than 30% of global vehicle production. In addition, China has already installed the capacity to produce 48 million vehicles per year.

In comparison, in 2024, the United States manufactured 10.6 million cars and trucks. This is less than one third of Chinese production.

American production is actually lower. Virtually all vehicles "made" in the United States are assembled, largely, from imported parts. At least 50% of the content of each "American made" vehicle is imported, usually from Mexico or Canada. Thus, U.S. vehicle production is at least half of what is commonly claimed. That would indicate that the United States is producing – at best – five million vehicles per year. That is about 10% of China's car-making capacity.

Let's look at the production of washing machines. In 2023, China produced 105 million sets of washing machines and dryers. That's the equivalent of one washing machine and dryer for every three people in the United States.

The United States, in comparison, relies on imported washing machines to meet most of its demand. The United States imports more washing machines than any other country in the world. In 2023, we imported $2.4 billion of domestic washing machines and dryers.

We can extend this comparison to virtually every product produced in the world today. China produces over 50% of the world's refrigerators, over 60% of televisions, 70% of solar cells, 80% of computers and air conditions, and 90% of cell phones. In each of these instances, the United States has minimal, if no production capacity. The United States would struggle to meet its own demand.

None of these numbers should be a surprise. China employs 162 million people in manufacturing. That is ten times larger than the American manufacturing workforce. China's factory population is also nearly three times larger than NATO's workforce, which is only about 62 million workers.

Now, we are starting to get an understanding of the relative size of the United States economy to the Chinese economy.

While China's population is 4.2 times larger than that of the United States, China is approximately 30 to 50 times more productive than the United States.

In other words, the productive capacity of the United States is a small fraction of China's productive capacity. China focuses on production. The United States focuses on consumption, which produces little, if anything of value.

If you live in the United States, you may be wondering if all of this matters.

On the surface, everything seems to be going well. Americans have money to spend. Our restaurants are flooded with people. Our shopping malls are filled with imported goods. We have new cars to buy, whether they are from Japan or Mexico. As Miley Cyrus says, there always seems to be a "Party in the U.S.A."

This book argues that American prosperity is largely an illusion, created by the way the world economy is set up. The standard of living in the United States is artificially sustained by our nation's control of the world's primary reserve currency – the dollar. It's easy to print dollars, and bring assets into the United States.

Let's take a look at how the dollar artificially boosts the standard of living in America. Let's start with our nation's twin deficits – the federal budget deficit and the trade deficit.

Federal budget deficit.

If you ever visit New York City, you can see the National Debt Clock. The clock keeps track of the cumulative debt of the United States government. The National Debt Clock is a billboard-sized digital display, showing the national debt on a real-time basis. The clock is located west of Sixth Avenue, between 42nd and 43rd Streets in New York City.

As of July 2025, the national debt was $37.1 trillion. That amounts to $108,310 per person in the United States, or $323,052 per taxpayer.

Since 1950, the United States has run a surplus only nine years. The remaining seventy-five years the government has run a deficit. The numbers are as follows:

Table 3.1

United States Federal Budget Deficit

Fiscal Year	Deficit ($billions)	Debt to GDP Ratio
1960	($1)	(0.05%)
1961	$3	0.61%
1962	$7	1.22%
1963	$5	0.77%
1964	$6	0.89%
1965	$1	0.20%
1966	$4	0.47%
1967	$9	1.03%
1968	$25	2.80%
1969	($3)	(0.33%)
1970	$3	0.27%
1971	$23	2.06%
1972	$23	1.92%
1973	$15	1.10%
1974	$6	0.41%
1975	$53	3.31%
1976	$74	4.13%
1977	$54	2.65%
1978	$59	2.60%
1979	$41	1.59%
1980	$74	2.64%
1981	$79	2.52%
1982	$128	3.86%

1983	$208	5.88%
1984	$185	4.69%
1985	$212	4.98%
1986	$221	4.89%
1987	$150	3.14%
1988	$155	3.12%
1989	$153	2.75%
1990	$221	3.75%
1991	$269	4.42%
1992	$290	4.52%
1993	$255	3.76%
1994	$203	2.83%
1995	$164	2.16%
1996	$107	1.35%
1997	$22	0.26%
1998	($69)	(0.77%)
1999	($126)	(1.33%)
2000	($236)	(2.34%)
2001	($128)	(1.22%)
2002	$158	1.46%
2003	$378	3.35%
2004	$413	3.43%
2005	$318	2.48%
2006	$248	1.82%
2007	$160	1.12%
2008	$459	3.10%
2009	$1,413	9.76%
2010	$1,294	8.70%

2011	$1,300	8.40%
2012	$1,077	6.68%
2013	$680	4.07%
2014	$484	2.78%
2015	$442	2.43%
2016	$585	3.13%
2017	$665	3.43%
2018	$779	3.81%
2019	$984	4.62%
2020	$3,132	14.71%
2021	$2,775	12.10%
2022	$1,376	5.44%
2023	$1,695	6.28%
2024	$1,833	6.40%

The above numbers indicate some important trends in the United States.

While the media tells us that the United States is rich, we can see that a large percentage of economy is actually borrowed. In the early 1970s, the federal government began to borrow about 2% of the size of the economy each year, to fund the government. This amount has grown steadily, to over 6% of GDP in 2024.

For some years, the numbers are particularly large. For example, during the Great Recession of 2009 through 2011, the United States borrowed between 8% and 10% of the entire economy. Things were even worse during the covid years. During 2020 and 2021, the federal government borrowed between 12% and 15% of the entire economy – an astonishing number.

However, even in good years, the United States government is dependent upon printed money. In 2023 and 2024, the Biden Administration printed 6.3% of the U.S. economy.

Typically, printing large amounts of money results in inflation. If there are more dollars chasing the same amount of goods, then the price of goods tends to go up.

For example, consider the case of Argentina. Between 2017 and 2020, Argentina ran a government deficit equal to between 6.1% and 8.5% of Argentine GDP. Between 2017 and 2020, Argentina experienced inflation of between 40% and 55% per year.

The United States has generally been able to avoid inflation at these levels, because the U.S. dollar is the world's reserve currency. If the United States prints $100 billion dollars, the world has been willing to accept those dollars. They end in bank accounts in Paris, London, Ottawa or the Caribbean. Since the dollars end up overseas, they don't end up producing large amounts of inflation in the United States – yet.

However, this trend is changing. The dollars used to end up in bank accounts in Moscow, Rio de Janeiro, and Beijing. However, these countries – Russia, Brazil and China – are expressing concerns about accepting America's dollars. More and more, they don't want the dollars. They would prefer to be paid in gold, or in the currency of stronger nations, such as China.

As the world reduces its acceptance of dollars, the United States will see increased inflation, due to our government's penchant for printing dollars. Inflation of 40% to 50% in the United States is possible. During the covid situation, in 2020 and 2021, the government increased the money supply by approximately 40% -- in just two years. During those two years, prices in the United States increased by about 40%. Just like that, everything went up – from groceries to real estate.

The important thing to remember is that inflation is a foreseeable result of too many dollars, chasing the same supply of goods. It will increase as our government continues to increase the money supply, and the world wants fewer of our dollars. More about that later in the book.

You may be asking – why would foreigners not want our dollars?

The answer is simple. There is a time bomb in the United States economy. As our government's debt increases, the interest payment on the debt also gets larger.

In 2024, our government paid $880 billion of interest on the national debt. That was higher than the amounts we spent on the next two largest categories in the federal budget – national defense and Medicare.

If the interest number gets too big, the United States could face a budget crisis. This typically happens when a nation's debt gets to about 120% of the size of that nation's economy. The United States is at that level today.

When a nation can't pay its debt, then the value of that country's currency tends to drop – often dramatically. This is known as a currency collapse.

Think about how a currency collapse could affect your life.

If the dollar falls 50% in value, then the price of goods imported into the United States would double. The cell phone that you paid $850 for, would now cost you $1,700. Remember, cell phones are not produced in the United States. Your $450 computer would now cost $900. Remember, computers are not produced in the United States. That large flat screen television, that you got on sale for $400, would now cost $800. And so on.

These numbers would be even worse, if the dollar fell by more than 50%. If the dollar fell by 75%, then the price of goods imported into the United States would increase by four times. Now, your $450 computer would cost $1,800. For many people, that would be too much. Overnight, our nation would become a poor country, because our nation could not afford personal computers. Remember, computers are made in other, wealthier countries – Japan, China and Korea.

A currency collapse would be devastating in the United States. As President Trump has said, if we lose the U.S. dollar, it would be same as losing a major war. By printing dollars with abandon, the foreseeable effect is that the dollar is going down.

Economists tell us that the United States is protected from a default on the national debt, because our nation's interest payments are denominated in U.S. dollars – which we can print. This is only a partial solution to the problem. While the United States can print dollars to pay its creditors, that only makes the debt larger. Eventually, fewer and fewer foreigners will want those dollars. The value of the dollar will drop, as the United States is choked in inflation. It's not a pretty picture. But that is the direction things are headed.

Trade deficit

If you have ever visited Trenton, New Jersey, you may have noticed a sign on a bridge over the Delaware River. The sign reads: "Trenton makes, the world takes."

Both the sign and its message date from a prior era. The sign was installed in 1917, when Trenton was a large manufacturing center.

For example, Trenton made the wire cables for the Brooklyn Bridge. Trenton made rails for the nation's railroads. In the 20th century,

Trenton produced rubber, plastics, metal works, electrical components, automobile parts, glass, and textiles.

Today, most of these factories are gone. Trenton's industrial economy faced the same fate as Detroit, Cleveland and Pittsburgh. The factories closed, and the machine tools were shipped overseas.

We can track this decline by looking at the balance of trade for the United States. The balance of trade tracks the flow of material goods in and out of the United States. Since 1970, our nation's balance of trade has turned sharply negative.

Table 3.2

United States Trade Balance

Year	Billions of US $	% of GDP
1970	$3.95	0.37%
1971	$0.62	0.05%
1972	$-3.37	-0.26%
1973	$4.11	0.29%
1974	$-0.82	-0.05%
1975	$15.98	0.95%
1976	$-1.63	-0.09%
1977	$-23.09	-1.11%
1978	$-25.37	-1.08%
1979	$-22.55	-0.86%
1980	$-13.06	-0.46%
1981	$-12.52	-0.39%
1982	$-19.97	-0.60%
1983	$-51.64	-1.42%
1984	$-102.73	-2.54%
1985	$-114.02	-2.63%

Year	Amount	Percent
1986	$-131.87	-2.88%
1987	$-144.77	-2.98%
1988	$-109.39	-2.09%
1989	$-86.74	-1.54%
1990	$-77.85	-1.31%
1991	$-28.61	-0.46%
1992	$-34.74	-0.53%
1993	$-65.17	-0.95%
1994	$-92.49	-1.27%
1995	$-89.76	-1.17%
1996	$-96.38	-1.19%
1997	$-101.97	-1.19%
1998	$-162.71	-1.80%
1999	$-259.55	-2.69%
2000	$-381.07	-3.72%
2001	$-376.75	-3.56%
2002	$-439.75	-4.02%
2003	$-521.96	-4.56%
2004	$-634.14	-5.19%
2005	$-739.90	-5.67%
2006	$-786.45	-5.69%
2007	$-735.93	-5.08%
2008	$-740.87	-5.02%
2009	$-419.15	-2.90%
2010	$-532.31	-3.54%
2011	$-579.62	-3.72%
2012	$-551.62	-3.39%
2013	$-479.39	-2.85%

2014	$-510.04	-2.91%
2015	$-526.20	-2.89%
2016	$-506.25	-2.71%
2017	$-539.93	-2.77%
2018	$-596.19	-2.90%
2019	$-596.26	-2.79%
2020	$-651.19	-3.12%
2021	$-845.05	-3.70%
2022	$-945.30	-3.70%
2023	$-773.40	-2.80%
2024	$-918.40	-3.10%

As we can see from the above chart, each year the United States imports manufactured goods equal to 3% to 4% of the nation's GDP.

When we add this number to the amount borrowed by the federal government (i.e. 6% of GDP), we find that about 10% of our nation's economy is borrowed, either through the government printing money or borrowed by financed trade.

The United States last ran a trade surplus in 1975 -- fifty years ago. Since 1975, our nation has run a structural trade deficit, that continues to grow.

If we add up all of America's trade deficits from 1976 through 2024, we learn that the United States has incurred a cumulative trade debt of $17.2 trillion.

You may be wondering – does that debt matter?

Consider our nation's trade debt for 2024. In 2024, we ran a trade deficit of $918 billion. That was enough money to purchase all of the gold in Fort Knox. It took our nation fifty years to acquire that gold, in the early 20th century.

In other words, each year, we – the American people –are transferring to our neighbors on the planet our cumulative national wealth. Over time, we are doing severe damage to our economy.

America for sale

In 1907, President Theodore Roosevelt laid the first stone for the Washington National Cathedral, in Washington, D.C. It would take eighty years to complete the building. Work was finally finished in 1990, when President George H.W. Bush laid the last stone.

The cathedral is a large Gothic structure, located on Mount Saint Alban, in our nation's capital. The building includes 112 gargoyles, and at least one stone that weighs five tons. The main tower of the edifice reaches 676 feet above sea level, making it the highest point in the District of Columbia.

One morning, in the early 1980s, the residents of Saint Alban woke up, and found that someone had hung a large "For Sale" sign on top of the cathedral's tower. The sign was hung from an area of the cathedral that was not accessible, either from the inside of the building or the outside. It would have taken rock climbing skills to reach the top of the tower, with the sign.

No one knew who placed the sign at the top of the cathedral.

The Washington Post wrote a cheeky article about the For Sale sign, suggesting that perhaps the sign was a political statement. After all, the sign was hung at the highest point in Washington, D.C. Presumably, the prankster was making a comment about the White House and Congress being for sale. The event was then forgotten, as the newspaper moved on to other topics.

Over the years, no one ever knew who hung the For Sale sign on the cathedral. Fewer and fewer people remembered the event.

Years later, a girlfriend told me that her brother hung the sign on the cathedral. She confirmed that he had used rock climbing equipment to get to the top of the building. Her brother then went on to an astonishing career in the United States media, rising to the highest levels of the economy.

By hanging the sign, my girlfriend's brother was making an apt statement -- not just about politics in Washington, D.C. He was also describing the reality of the United States economy, under the existing system. America's assets are literally for sale.

When the United States runs a deficit in international trade – as it has done for the last fifty years – the United States loses power and wealth. To cover the deficit, the United States must transfer assets to the creditor nation, to cover the goods that are not paid for. As a result, we, as a nation, no longer own important assets in our own country.

In the 1980s, a Japanese company bought Rockefeller Center, in New York. Americans were horrified that their former enemy, the Japanese, now controlled an American icon.

The transaction, however, was just a consequence of America's trade deficit with Japan. Americans loved Toyota and Honda cars, and the cars needed to be paid for. The United States was not willing to transfer gold to Japan. Instead, we gave them Rockefeller Center. The Japanese were willing to take the building, in return for their cars.

Now, multiply the Rockefeller Center deal by hundreds of times, and you begin to see the effect of the nation's trade deficit on our economy. These deals have become so common, that they are no longer scandalous in the media.

Our auto company, Chrysler, was sold to a Dutch owner, after merging with Italian Fiat. AB Electrolux, of Sweden, bought Frigidaire. Nestlé, a Swiss company, purchased Stouffers. An investor from Dubai purchased the Los Angeles Dodgers. Presumably, he wanted to be paid for his oil. AB InBev, a Belgium company, purchased Anheuser Busch. Tiffany & Company went to LVMH, a French company.

The Chinese – swimming in American-printed dollars – have acquired numerous U.S. assets. In 2014, a Chinese insurance company bought the Waldorf Astoria in New York. At the time, no one blinked. That same year, Lenovo, a Chinese company, bought Motorola.

Lenovo also purchased IBM's personal computer division, in 2005. This included the ThinkPad line of computers. In 2016, Haier Group, a Chinese appliance company, bought GE Appliances.

China is also making in-roads in the American media environment. In 2012, China's Dalian Wanda Group acquired the movie chain, AMC. After the deal closed, AMC purchased Carmike Cinemas, for an additional $1.2 billion. Thus, China now has a large say on what types of movies you get to watch in America.

China is also acquiring important assets in the U.S. food supply. In 2013, WMH Group, a Chinese company, paid $7.3 billion to purchase Smithfield Foods. Smithfield Foods owns large amounts of American farm land, raising questions as to where our nation's food supply will be sent in the future.

As we saw with the Smithfield Foods deal, our nation's security is beginning to suffer. For example, consider U.S. Steel Corporation. During the First and Second World Wars, U.S. Steel produced hundreds of millions of tons of steel for the war effort. Even today, U.S. Steel produces about 20% of domestic steel production.

In 2025, the United States transferred ownership of U.S. Steel to a Japanese corporation. The World War II generation – which is mostly no longer alive – would be shocked. However, the United States had no choice. Our country no longer had the capital or the technology necessary to allow U.S. Steel to thrive.

The same thing happened with the Philadelphia Shipyard. During World War II, the Philadelphia Shipyard employed 40,000 workers building and repairing battleships, cruisers and destroyers. Most notably, the Philadelphia Shipyard produced the battleship New Jersey, and its sister ship, the U.S.S. Wisconsin. In 2024, our nation sold the shipyard to South Korea's Hanwha Group. The United States no longer had the capital or the technology necessary for the business.

Are you starting to see the writing on the wall?

America is becoming a poor country – because of our nation's cumulative trade deficit. We can't profitably sell goods overseas, so we are having to transfer assets to pay for our purchases of foreign goods.

Both U.S. Steel and the Philadelphia Shipyard have machine tools that are now, in the hands of foreigners. Modern machine tools are often operated by means of computer systems. These computer systems can be locked, by means of electronic passwords. As a result, foreigners now have the ability to shut down U.S. production in key areas of national defense. This includes 20% of our nation's steel production, as well as a key shipyard on the east coast.

This is a real concern. For example, the United States no longer has the ability to make large cranes for moving cargo at ports. For many years, the United States has imported cranes for our shipyards. Many of these cranes were manufactured in China.

During the Biden administration, the U.S. government began to view Chinese production of these cranes as a security threat. China could easily install a "kill switch" in every crane installed in the United States. This would allow China to remotely shut down any port using its equipment.

In addition, some of the Chinese-made cranes use sophisticated sensors, which can track the origin and destination of shipping containers. The Pentagon has identified this as a security risk, because China will know where our shipments are going. According to the Wall Street Journal, the military has taken steps to avoid ports that use these Chinese-produced cranes.

In 2024, the federal government decided to spend $20 billion to remove the Chinese-made cranes from U.S. ports. The cranes will be replaced with cranes produced by a joint United States-Japanese company.

Thus, the trade deficit is starting to create national security risks for the United States. However, the cumulative trade deficit poses other risks as well. With each dollar transferred overseas, the United

States loses the ability to defend the value of the dollar, vis-à-vis other currencies.

U.S. Foreign Currency Reserves are Dwindling

On February 3, 2025, President Trump announced the creation of a Sovereign Wealth Fund for the United States. The idea of a sovereign wealth fund is a good one. Many countries use sovereign wealth funds to invest national savings, to obtain a better return and to help achieve the nation's objectives.

A sovereign wealth fund can also defend a nation's currency, in the event of a balance of payments crisis.

For example, in 1997, the world experienced the Asian Financial Crisis. The crisis started in Thailand, in May 1997. As a result of heavy international debt, the Thai currency – known as the baht – came under pressure. Foreigners were dumping the Thai baht, because they believed that the currency would fall in value, due to Thailand's large foreign debt.

Thailand could not afford to defend the currency. Doing so would have required Thailand to have a large amount of foreign currency reserves – which Thailand did not have. As a result, Thailand allowed the baht to float freely on world markets, subject to supply and demand.

By January 1998, the Thai baht dropped from 25 to 56 to the dollar. This was a devaluation of over 100%, causing prices of imported goods in Thailand to double overnight. Thailand's ability to consume foreign goods was cut in half. The Thai stock market dropped 75%, and poverty increased significantly in Thailand.

The financial crisis quickly spread to other countries that had high levels of foreign debt. These included Malaysia, Indonesia and Russia. All experienced financial distress, as the value of their currencies fell.

Richer regions, such as Hong Kong, were able to avoid the crisis altogether. In October 1997, the Hong Kong dollar came under speculative pressure. At that time, Hong Kong pegged its dollar at 7.8 to one U.S. dollar.

Hong Kong was able to defend the currency peg, because the city-state was rich – it had more than $80 billion in foreign currency reserves.

When foreign hedge funds began dumping the Hong Kong dollar looking for profit, Hong Kong's finance ministry responded in kind. Hong Kong spent $1 billion of its foreign reserves to purchase Hong Kong dollars. The foreign hedge funds were burned. Hong Kong was able to defend the currency peg, and avert the crisis.

Thus, sovereign wealth funds play an important role in defending a nation's currency.

However, a sovereign wealth fund requires a nation to run a profit, in foreign trade. If a nation runs a trade deficit, then there is no money to put in the fund. In addition, there is no money to defend that nation's currency. As we saw in the case of Thailand, in 1997, the currency falls, and the nation is plunged into poverty.

President Trump has been trying to drum up money for his sovereign wealth fund. This will not be easy to do, given that "America, Inc." has not run a profit in the last half century.

As we have seen, since 1975, the United States has lost $17.2 trillion dollars, in foreign trade. As a result, the United States has few foreign currency reserves to place in a sovereign wealth fund.

Let's take stock of America's national assets, and consider whether those assets are sufficient to defend the United States dollar.

Our nation's best foreign reserve asset is our stock of gold.

During the first half of the 20th century, the United States ran large trade surpluses. As we have seen, during this time, our nation provided large amounts of food, weapons, ammunition and clothing to the powers in Europe. Britain, in particular, paid us with large amounts of gold.

By 1941, the United States owned over 20,000 metric tons of gold. This was 80% of the gold reserves held by the world's central banks. In the last eighty years, the United States has lost over half of this gold, by running trade deficits. Today, our gold reserves are about 40% of this number.

According to the Department of Treasury, the United States now owns 8,133 metric tons of gold. This gold is stored at the Federal Reserve Bank in New York; Fort Knox; West Point; and in Denver, Colorado.

If we multiply this number by a recent price of gold – $3,350 per troy ounce as of July 2025 – we learn that the United States owns $876 billion worth of gold. That is less than $1 trillion dollars. That is not enough to cover a single year of America's trade deficit – which is about $900 billion per year.

What else can we put in the Sovereign Wealth Fund?

According to the Department of Treasury, the United States also owns a small amount of foreign currencies, bonds, and other assets. As of July 2025, the United States owned $243.3 billion worth of following reserve assets:

Table 3.3

United States Foreign Currency Reserves

Asset	Value in Dollars (billions) (as of July 11, 2025)
Euro	$14.0
Yen	$7.2
Foreign Bonds	$17.7
IMF Reserves	$30.2
SDRs	$174.2
TOTAL	$243.3

Thus, besides gold, the United States has about a quarter billion dollars of liquid foreign assets. Together with the gold, we have about $1.1 billion of foreign currency reserves.

President Trump has suggested adding crypto currencies to the mix. President Trump has appointed David Sacks to serve as a "cryptocurrency czar," to supervise this initiative. According to Mr. Sacks, federal agencies have seized about 200,000 bitcoin, from suspected drug dealers. This stash is worth about $23.5 billion at the current price. However, Sacks cautions that "there has never been a complete audit."

If we add the confiscated bitcoin to the above assets, we find that the United States has the following immediately marketable assets, as of July 2025:

Table 3.4

United States Reserve Assets

Type of Asset	Amount
Gold	$876 billion
Reserve Assets	$243 billion
Crypto Currency	$23 billion
TOTAL	$1,142 billion

That gives the United States about $1.1 trillion of immediately marketable assets.

Of course, the United States owns millions of acres of land, thousands of buildings, and hundreds of Navy ships. However, the federal government cannot easily liquidate these holdings, to ensure America's solvency.

Let's consider how America's proposed Sovereign Wealth Fund compares to other nations' funds. As of early 2025, the following countries had roughly the following amount of reserve assets:

Table 3.5

World Reserve Assets

Country	Assets ($ Trillions)
China	$3.45
Japan	$1.30
United States	$1.10
Switzerland	$0.86
India	$0.63
Russia	$0.60

Taiwan	$0.49
Saudi Arabia	$0.46
South Korea	$0.42
Singapore	$0.36
Brazil	$0.36
Germany	$0.32
Italy	$0.25
France	$0.24
Thailand	$0.22
Mexico	$0.21
Israel	$0.20
Poland	$0.19
U.A.E.	$0.19
United Kingdom	$0.18

Thus, as of 2025, the United States remains the third wealthiest country in the world, in terms of reserve assets. While we have $1.1 trillion, China is three times wealthier, in terms of reserve assets.

In reality, as of 2025, the United States has one additional asset that makes the United States – for time being – richer than China.

That is our ability to print U.S. dollars.

As of 2025, the U.S. dollar is convertible to oil. Thus, the United States could, in theory, print $2 trillion U.S. dollars, and purchase $2 trillion of gold, euro, Japanese yen, or Chinese yuan. Then suddenly – overnight – the United States would have as much foreign currency reserves as China.

Can this be done? Yes, and the United States does it routinely.

Consider, for example, the covid years. During 2020 and 2021, the federal government borrowed the following amounts:

Table 3.6

Federal Deficit During Covid

Fiscal Year	Deficit ($ billions)	Debt to GDP Ratio
2020	$3,132	14.71%
2021	$2,775	12.10%

In those two years alone, the U.S. government borrowed nearly $6 trillion dollars. This was five times the amount of America's reserve assets of $1.1 trillion.

However, in 2021, the United States was not interested in purchasing reserve assets. Instead, our nation was interested in purchasing goods from Asia. We wanted new computers, new kitchens with fancy gadgets, flat screen televisions from South Korea. We wanted cars, cell phones, refrigerators, and all of those lovely things that factories in Asia are so good at producing.

Like Aladdin's magic lamp, a fleet of ships appeared on America's west coast, and delivered trillions of dollars of extra goods.

These extra goods swamped our nation's ports. The backlog was astonishing. The number of container ships waiting to unload in Los Angeles and Long Beach peaked in February 2022, with 150 ships offshore. Other ports, such as Savannah, Georgia, also experienced significant delays.

The media portrayed these delays as having been caused by covid-19. They led us to believe that the dock workers were home, staying quarantined.

However, the delays were actually caused by the rapid increase in the U.S. dollar money supply. In 2020 and 2021, during covid, the United States increased the money supply by 40%, or $6 trillion.

That $6 trillion choked the nation's ports.

The United States does this all of the time with wars. If we need to place an army in the Middle East, the government simply prints a trillion dollars, and poof, the army appears. This is how the United States fought the war in Iraq, in the early 2000s.

Since 2023, the United States has printed dollars to fight the war in Ukraine, against Russia. If the United States needs artillery shells from South Korea or Australia, we simply print the dollars, and magically, the 155mm shells appear on our shores.

If the United States needs to move microchip factories back from Taiwan, to avoid Chinese control, then the United States simply prints $500 billion. And magically, chip factories appear in Arizona, Texas and Ohio.

Everyone wants U.S. dollars. Those dollars have value. They are accepted all over the world, because the U.S. dollar is the world's primary reserve currency.

If America is smart, it will print an extra trillion dollars, or two, and fund President Trump's new Sovereign Wealth Fund. Ideally, America should purchase gold with those extra dollars. However, euro, yen, Chinese yuan would be good too. It would save the American people years, if they had to work for that money.

By now, you may be asking another question:

How is it possible that the United States can create real goods out of thin air, simply by printing dollars?

Other nations do not have this power. When they print their currency, they get inflation. When the United States prints dollars, we get new cars and refrigerators.

To answer this question, we have to look at the history of the international trade system, as it was set up after the Second World War. The people who set up the system knew what they were doing. They were Americans seeking an advantage for the United States.

However, the system that they set up was fundamentally flawed. The system is unstable, and could create severe problems for the United States in the near future.

CHAPTER 4

Dueling Views of The Dollar

In order to understand the precarious nature of the dollar, it is useful to quickly review the history of money. The history of money is like watching a shell game on the streets of New York. Money starts out as something tangible, having value. However, when you are not looking, that value can quickly disappear.

Let's start with societies where money had tangible value.

For example, ancient Rome used salt as money. Salt was ideal to use as a currency. It was scarce, because it had to be mined, and transported many miles to its destination. It is also useful. Salt enhances the flavor of food, and preserves meat. At a medieval feast, you had great rank if you sat near the salt. No need to say pass the salt.

As times changed, the form of money also changed. In North America, in the 1600s, the early explorers used beaver pelts and buckskins as a form of money. In Canada, the Hudson Bay Company established a fixed barter system, based on beaver pelts:

    5 pounds of sugar cost 1 beaver pelt
    2 scissors cost 1 beaver pelt
    20 fish hooks cost 1 beaver pelt

1 pair of shoes cost 1 beaver pelt
1 gun cost 12 beaver pelts

And of course, gold and silver have served as money for thousands of years. When explorer Howard Carter discovered King Tut's tomb in 1922 in Egypt's Valley of the Kings, he found pounds of gold inside. The gold had not lost its luster, or value, in 3,000 years.

The Roman Empire made widespread use of both gold and silver coins. The Roman emperor, Nero, began the practice of debasing the metal content of the coins. Nero governed the Roman empire between 54 and 68 AD. During these years, he reduced the silver content of the denarius coin to 3.4 grams. During the third century AD, the Roman empire began making coins out of copper. The silver content of some coins fell to only 2% of the coin. This caused widespread inflation, which disrupted the monetary system.

In AD 310, Roman Emperor Constantine decided to restore credibility to the currency. Constantine issued a new gold coin, called the solidus. Constantine declared that the weight of the solidus would be constant, at 4.55 grams of gold, and that its weight should not be reduced. The solidus lasted for a thousand years, until the fall of Constantinople to the Ottoman Turks in 1453.

The gold standard v. the urge to print

In the Middle Ages, the world's bankers discovered that they could create "gold" out of thin air, by issuing promissory notes representing a portion of gold in a vault.

Suppose a banker had 200 pounds of gold in a vault. The banker could get value for that gold, by creating a written document promising to deliver a certain amount of gold on demand, to whoever possessed the document. Everyone thought that this was a great idea. The gold sat secure in the vault. And the promissory note weighed much less than a heavy bag of gold or silver coins. In addition, if the note was payable to a certain person, then the note itself was secure from theft. This was the introduction of paper money.

However, paper money created a moral hazard. If the bank had $100,000 of gold in the vault from depositors, there was an incentive on the part of the bank to issue paper notes in excess of the value of the gold in the vault. Few people knew how much gold was in the bank. A clever banker could quickly turn $100,000 of gold into $500,000, with a few strokes of a pen. This was an easy way to rapidly multiply one's money.

The system worked until the bank's depositors got uneasy, and came looking for their gold. This would create a "run on the bank," which rarely ended happily for those who had entrusted their gold to the bank.

The use of gold and silver as a measure of currency carried over to the early United States. On October 15, 1794, the United States coined its first silver dollars in Philadelphia. The coin was modeled on the Spanish silver dollar -- commonly known as pieces of eight. The U.S. dollar was defined as 26.96 grams of silver.

The U.S. mint issued its first gold coins the following year, in 1795. These were the Eagle, worth $10; the Half Eagle, worth $5; and the Quarter Eagle, worth $2.50.

For many years, the U.S. dollar was firmly pegged to gold. In 1834, the United States decided that one ounce of gold would be worth $20.67 U.S. dollars. This meant that one dollar was worth approximately 5% of an ounce of gold.

The United States was able to maintain this ratio of gold to dollars for a surprisingly long time. This is because the gold supply in the United States grew rapidly in the 19th century. In 1848, gold was discovered in California. The resulting Gold Rush caused a massive influx of gold into the U.S. economy.

Between 1870 and 1914, most industrialized nations tied their currencies to gold. These included Britain, France, Germany, Italy and Spain. This period was known as the Classic Gold Standard.

The gold standard began to break down in 1914, with the outbreak of the First World War. With the onset of war, Britain, France and Germany needed to print large amounts of money to pay for the war. This could not be done with the British pound and French franc tied to gold.

Britain suspended the convertibility of the British pound to gold at the outbreak of the war. France, Germany and Italy abandoned the gold standard at the same time.

The suspension of the gold standard enabled the European powers to print large amounts of currency during the war. Britain experienced significant inflation during the conflict. Prices rose about 14% per year, between 1914 and the end of the war in 1919. Inflation was higher elsewhere. France, Holland, and Italy experienced inflation of over 30 percent per year during the war.

The United States did not abandon the gold standard during the war. Throughout the war, the United States maintained the ratio of $20.67 dollars to one once of gold. This was an astonishing achievement, given that the United States also needed to print large amounts of money to finance its own war effort.

The United States entered the war in April 1917. The United States was able to maintain the convertibility of the dollar to gold, because large amounts of gold were flowing into the United States. For much of the war, our nation sold goods to both sides of the conflict. The British and Germans paid for these goods, in part, in gold.

By the end of the war, the world began to view the U.S. dollar as being as "good as gold." The United States dollar was the new gold standard.

When the war ended in 1918, Europe did not immediately return to the gold standard. The European economies were a mess, due to the war. Germany was on the verge of famine, and large parts of France were destroyed by the fighting. It was necessary to quickly demobilize the armies, and get people back to work. This meant printing more currency, to keep the European economies alive.

After the war, Britain and France forced Germany to pay reparations of 132 billion German marks. This was equal to about $605 billion in 2025 dollars – a significant amount for Germany's economy, which was much smaller a century ago.

Germany had no ability to pay France and Britain reparations. As a result, Germany printed large amounts of money.

In August 1921, Germany's central bank began buying hard currency at any price. Germany's central bank printed German marks to purchase British pounds and French francs. Germany claimed that this was necessary to make reparations payments.

In early 1922, Germany began to experience hyperinflation from the central bank's printing. The value of the German mark fell from 320 marks per dollar in mid-1922 to 7,400 marks per U.S. dollar six months later, in December 1922. This was a devaluation of approximately 96%, in the value of the mark.

In 1923, the hyperinflation only got worse. By November 1923, one U.S. dollar was worth 4.2 trillion marks. Needless to say, this printing created havoc in Germany. The rapid devaluation of the German mark caused prices to soar. Savings accounts became worthless. People were forced to barter for goods. This economic instability caused political instability, which contributed to the rise of Nazism a decade later.

Between 1925 and 1931, Western Europe made an effort to restore the gold standard. During this time, Britain and France restored the convertibility of their currencies to gold.

The new system became known as the "Gold Exchange Standard." Under this system, the United States and the United Kingdom held their reserves strictly in gold. Other countries, which could not afford large amounts of gold, held their reserves in either gold or other nation's currencies. The world was starting to move towards the modern system of numerous paper currencies, issued by many nations.

However, the genie was out of the bottle. Britain and France liked the ease of printing paper money, without the need to actually hold gold in a vault. They continued to print, even though their currencies were still theoretically convertible to gold.

In 1931, Britain abandoned the gold standard a second time. The British pound immediately fell by 30%. The devaluation made British goods significantly cheaper on world markets. The pound continued to fall in value throughout the 1930s, eventually reaching approximately half of its former value by 1940. As a result of these moves, the British economy became significantly more competitive.

Britain's devaluation forced other countries to also abandon the gold standard -- and to engage in competitive devaluations. By the end of 1931, twenty-three countries had left the gold standard.

The United States initially held on, and maintained the convertibility of the dollar to gold. However, pressure from other countries was too great.

In 1933, large amounts of gold began to flow out of the United States. This indicated that investors believed that the dollar was overvalued, and would soon be devalued against gold. Investors wanted gold, rather than dollars.

On April 5, 1933, U.S. President Franklin Roosevelt banned private ownership of gold in the United States. Roosevelt's order required individuals to deliver their gold to the Federal Reserve by May 1, 1933, at an exchange rate of $20.67 per ounce. This was the same price set by the United States for gold in 1834. The gold exchange ratio had held for a century.

On April 20, 1933, Roosevelt announced that the United States was leaving the gold standard. In other words, the United States would no longer provide gold to persons holding U.S. dollars. The United States was out of the gold business. To protect America's gold supply, Roosevelt prohibited the export of gold from the United States. These actions halted the gold outflows.

In October 1933, Roosevelt started the process of devaluing the dollar. He did this in very clever way. Roosevelt authorized a U.S. agency, the Reconstruction Finance Corporation (RFC), to purchase gold at progressively higher prices. The program was known as the Gold Purchase Plan, or the Warran Plan. In October 1933, the RFC paid $31.35 for an ounce of gold. This was substantially higher than the former price, of $21.67 per ounce.

This had the effect of devaluing the dollar against other major currencies, who looked to the price of gold to determine their value. The October 1933 price for gold, paid by the RFC, had the effect of devaluing the dollar by 44.6%.

The RFC gradually increased the price it would pay for gold. By January 1934, the agency was paying $35.00 an ounce. This represented a cumulative 61.5% devaluation of the dollar. The devaluation made U.S. goods competitive in world markets, vis-à-vis the nation's competitors.

Altogether, more than seventy countries devalued their currencies between 1929 and 1936. This was known as a currency war, and no country was completely happy with the results. In the late 1930s, Britain, France and the United States engaged in negotiations to stabilize world currencies. However, they were not successful in doing so.

The Second World War began on September 1, 1939, when Germany invaded Poland. For the next six years, the warring nations printed large amounts of their currencies to finance the second round of the ongoing war.

By 1944, it became clear that Britain and the United States were going to win the war. It was time to consider a new monetary system to replace the old method of competitive devaluations.

Bretton Woods -- the New Gold Standard

In July 1944, the United States held an international conference at Bretton Woods, New Hampshire to discuss a new monetary system. Delegates from 44 countries attended the conference. However, the conversation was dominated by the United States and Britain.

Britain had a voice at the conference because it still controlled the British Empire. At its peak, in about 1920, Britain controlled 25% of the earth's land mass. However, by 1944, Britain was physically and economically exhausted by the war with Germany.

The United States, on the other hand, was the new world power. The United States had avoided destruction during the wars. The United States held most of the world's gold reserves. As a result, America had both the factories and money to determine the rules for the new world order.

Economist John Maynard Keynes represented Britain at Bretton Woods. Keynes was arguably the most influential economist of the time. In 1936, he had published The General Theory of Employment, Interest and Money, which argued that governments should play a role in managing the economy.

The United States was represented at the conference by Henry Morgenthau Jr., Fred Vinson, Dean Acheson, and Harry Dexter White. Of these four, Harry Dexter White served as the primary architect of the new monetary system.

White suggested a system where the U.S. dollar would be convertible to a fixed price of gold. That price was the pre-war price of $35 per ounce. Other countries' currencies would be convertible for a fixed number of dollars, but would not be convertible to gold. The system was designed to provide stability, with countries discouraged from devaluing.

Keynes, speaking on behalf of Britain, objected to the proposed system. If the world used the dollar as the primary reserve currency, then a significant amount of international trade would be done in U.S.

dollars. If commodities, such as oil, were priced in dollars, then the United States would be able to get goods for free. It could do this by printing dollars, and then purchase the commodities for the printed dollars.

Keynes explained that White's proposed system put Britain at a disadvantage. If commodities were priced in dollars, then Britain would have to trade physical goods to obtain dollars, to purchase the commodities.

To make the system fair, Keynes proposed a new currency unit, which he called the Bancor. According to Keynes' proposal, an international organization known as the International Clearing Union would issue Bancor on behalf of the international community. The Clearing Union would be responsible for dealing with balances of payments between nations. Trade balances would be settled in Bancor, rather than gold or national currency.

If a country had a persistent trade deficit, then that county could devalue its currency, in terms of Bancor. If a country had a persistent trade surplus, then that country's currency would become more expensive, vis-à-vis the price of Bancor. In this way, Keynes proposed to ensure that international trade would remain balanced.

Keynes' proposal likely created anxiety for the United States delegation. In 1944, the United States was running a large trade surplus. Under no circumstances was the United States going to allow its currency to appreciate – i.e. become more expensive – to reduce the amount of that surplus. Furthermore, under no circumstances was the United States going to hand power over its own currency to a group of foreigners, whom the United States then dominated militarily and economically.

The United States won the debate, and the conference adopted White's proposed structure for the world economy. The Bancor idea was never adopted.

As of today, Keynes' proposal of a world currency remains an out of the box solution to a problem that continues to vex the world today – namely, the over-issuance of a reserve currency. When the reserve currency is placed in the hands of one nation, that nation has an economic incentive to issue too many currency units, causing others to lose faith in that currency. As a result, the value of that currency will collapse.

Keynes died less than two years later, in April 1946. However, his idea of an international currency unit continues to intrigue economists today.

Robert Triffin sounds the alarm.

The United States emerged victorious in August 1945, as the world's dominant economic, military and technological power.

After Bretton Woods, the United States now controlled the world's primary reserve currency. Increasingly, commodities – such as oil and wheat – were priced in U.S. dollars. This gave the United States the ability buy these commodities at little cost to America.

In theory, the dollar was still chained to the price of gold. For every $35 dollars that the United States printed, the government was expected to have one ounce of gold held in reserve. In practice, it didn't turn out that way.

Shortly after the war, both Britain and France were forced to devalue their currencies. In 1949, the French devalued the franc from 119.1 to 350 to the dollar. This was a 66% devaluation, in the value of the franc.

The devaluation made French goods 66% cheaper in world markets. Americans could now purchase nearly three times as much French goods, for the same price. Meanwhile, U.S. goods tripled in price in Paris.

Britain, too, was forced to devalue. In 1949, Britain devalued the pound from $4.03 to the pound, to $2.80 to the pound – a 30% reduction.

Soon American dollars were flowing to Europe. These dollars provided much needed relief for the war-torn economies of Britain, France and Germany.

Much of America's spending in Europe was military-related. In 1945, the United States had over 3 million service personnel in Europe. When the war ended, the United States rapidly demobilized the troops. Troop levels fell to as low of 79,000 in 1949. At that time, the United States felt comfortable that it could defend Western Europe, because it had a monopoly on atomic weapons.

In August 1949, the Soviet Union exploded its first atomic bomb. The detonation created panic among the political leaders in the United States. In 1949, the United States began to increase troop levels in Europe. The numbers reached 257,000 in 1952. By the late 1950s, the United States had over 400,000 troops in Europe.

America's defense spending had an effect on the nation's balance of payments. Between 1946 and 1949, the United States had a balance of payments surplus of $2 billion per year. Between 1950 and 1956, the trade balance went negative, with the United States incurring a loss of $1.5 billion per year, in 1950s dollars.

In the late 1950s, the deficits increased. From 1958 to 1960, the United States incurred average trade deficits of $3.8 billion per year. This would be equal to about $42 billion in today's money.

As dollars piled up overseas, European nations began to redeem the dollars for gold. Gold began to flow out of the United States. Between 1949 and 1959, U.S. gold holdings dropped from $24.4 billion to $19.7 billion – a 19% drop. This set off alarm bells with American policy makers.

In 1959, Yale economist, Robert Triffin, warned the U.S. Congress of serious flaws in the Bretton Woods system. Triffin testified that the United States was printing too many dollars, to support the convertibility of the dollar to gold at $35 per ounce. He told Congress that the United States would eventually have to devalue the dollar against gold, to continue convertibility. He predicted that the United States would have to abandon the gold standard.

In his book, Gold and the Dollar Crisis, published in 1960, Triffin warned of an even greater problem. By flooding world markets with dollars, the United States was providing "liquidity" for the world economy. Liquidity is the ease with which an asset can be converted into cash without affecting its market price. If the United States flooded Europe with dollars, then it was easier to buy and sell things in Europe with dollars, from real estate to a cup of coffee at the café. This liquidity allowed the world economy to grow, in both Western Europe and in Asia. This, on its face, was a good thing.

However, liquidity was a double-edged sword. On one hand, the United States was boosting world prosperity by allowing the world to engage in U.S. dollar transactions. On the other hand, the United States was incurring ever-larger trade deficits. This meant that the system was unsustainable. Eventually, the deficits would undermine confidence in the U.S. dollar, causing the value of the dollar to fall.

In coming to this conclusion, Triffin looked back at the history of the prior reserve currency – the British pound. He noted that Britain had been forced to abandon the gold standard in 1931. When Britain did so, the value of the pound fell by 28%. Triffin also noted the subsequent devaluation of the British pound in 1949, by an additional 30%. Triffin emphasized that the value of a currency cannot be sustained – no matter how strong – in light of unrestricted printing.

Triffin's warning became known as the "Triffin Dilemma." The Triffin Dilemma states that the United States cannot provide the primary reserve currency to the world indefinitely. To provide the reserve currency, the United States must run a balance of payments deficit. This is necessary to provide liquidity for the world economy. Eventually, America's cumulative deficits will undermine confidence in the dollar, causing the value of the dollar to fall, or possibly, collapse.

Triffin's solution to the dilemma was similar to that proposed by John Maynard Keynes, fifteen years earlier at the Bretton Woods

Conference. At Bretton Woods, as we have seen, Keynes suggested using an international currency – known as the Bancor – to provide liquidity for the world economy. The Bancor would have eliminated the incentive for any one country to issue large amounts of its currency, in the world economy. Triffin suggested a similar solution. He wrote:

> The most promising line of approach to a long-term solution to the problem lies in the true "internationalization" of the foreign exchange component of the world's international reserves, protecting the world monetary system from the instability resulting from arbitrary shifts from one reserve currency into another or into gold.

He suggested that an international body issue a new reserve asset, which would alleviate pressure upon the United States to run trade deficits.

The United States was not in favor of a new reserve asset. In the opinion of the U.S. Treasury Department, the U.S. dollar was the only reserve asset the world needed.

Triffin who was Belgian, and reached out to France for support. He wrote letters to French President, Charles De Gaulle, asking that France support his proposed policies to limit the growth of U.S. trade deficits. Triffin began to gain support in Europe.

Robert Roosa pitches the reserve currency.

In the early 1960s, President John Kennedy was very concerned about the increasing trade deficits affecting the United States. Kennedy was watching the U.S. gold reserves drop, and needed a solution. However, he and his government were not prepared to accept an international currency. That was too confusing, and gave away too much power. Kennedy preferred to keep the United States on course, with the dollar as the world's primary reserve currency.

However, the laws of economics were making things difficult for the Bretton Woods plan. In the early 1960s, the price of gold in London began to increase over $35 an ounce. Dollars were piling up in Europe, putting pressure on asset prices. By the fall of 1960, the price of gold in London was sometimes reaching $40 an ounce.

The United States tried to defend the Bretton Woods price, of $35 an ounce for gold. The point-person for this campaign was Robert V. Roosa, the Undersecretary of the Treasury for Currency Affairs in the Kennedy administration.

Roosa led an effort to suppress the price of gold in London. His plan became known as the London Gold Pool.

On November 1, 1961, the United States entered into an agreement with seven European central banks, to defend the price of gold established by the Bretton Woods agreement. The objective of the agreement was to maintain the price of gold, at $35 an ounce. Each country agreed to contribute a certain amount of gold to a pool, that would be used to supply the London gold market. The United States agreed to provide 50% of the gold. The remaining 50% came from West Germany, Britain, France, Italy, Belgium, the Netherlands, and Switzerland. When the price of gold got expensive, the pool would supply gold to the London market, to keep the price down. After gold was sold, the pool would theoretically repurchase the gold, when the price dropped.

The scheme proved to be unsustainable. By 1965, the pool could no longer repurchase gold at prices less than $35 an ounce. The gold pool began to run losses. By the mid-1960s, the cumulative deficit reached $3 billion, in 1960s dollars.

France objects to the gold pool.

The French Finance Minister, Valéry Giscard d'Estaing, suggested that American printing of dollars was the problem with the price of gold. D'Estaing complained that the dollar was an "exorbitant privilege" of the Americans. He felt that the United States was getting goods for free, because the United States paid for French goods in dollars, which only the United States could print. In making these comments, D'Estaing echoed the objections of economist Robert Triffin.

On February 4, 1965, the President of France – Charles de Gaulle – announced that France would exchange its U.S. dollar reserves for gold at the official exchange rate of $35 an ounce. De Gaulle was no fool. He knew that gold was worth more than $35 an ounce. He was happy to hold the Americans to their agreement, at Bretton Woods, to sell gold at $5 less than fair market value.

During the press conference, De Gaulle made clear that he thought it was a mistake for nations to accept unlimited payments of paper dollars from the United States. He said:

> The fact that many countries accept as a principle, dollars being as good as gold for the payment of the ... American balance of trade, this very fact, leads Americans to get into debt, and to get into debt for free, at the expense of other countries. Because, what the US owes them, it is paid, at least in part, with dollars [which] they are the only [ones] allowed to emit. Considering the serious consequences a crisis would have in such a domain, we think that measures must be taken on time to avoid it.

De Gaulle suggested returning to a gold standard, to ensure that nations settled their balance of trade with real assets, on a periodic basis.

The French president also insisted on the return to France of more than 3,000 tons of gold, which had been in New York for safe keeping since World War II. De Gaulle proposed sending a French navy vessel across the Atlantic, to pick up the gold reserves. He eventually agreed to ship the gold by Air France flights and commercial ships.

France's demands led to a run on the United States gold reserves. Other nations, such as the Netherlands, made similar demands to redeem their dollars.

In June 1967, France withdrew from the London Gold Pool. In March 1968, the system collapsed.

By the late 1960s, American options were dwindling. The U.S. dollar was still tied to the price of gold, at $35 per ounce. However, increasingly, the U.S. government was not willing to redeem U.S. dollars for gold, at that price or any other price.

Meanwhile, the United States continued to flood the world with dollars. In 1967, U.S. President Lyndon Johnson was ramping up America's war in Vietnam. By 1968, the United States had 543,000 troops in South Vietnam. This troop level was putting pressure on the dollar. These dollars were bidding up the price of assets worldwide, including the price of gold.

In 1969, the United States decided to reconsider Triffin's idea of setting up a new reserve asset, to alleviate pressure on the dollar. In that year, the International Monetary Fund issued a reserve asset known as the Special Drawing Right or "SDR". In theory, the SDR was meant to provide liquidity to the world economy, without the need for the United States to print dollars. However, in practice, the SDR did not solve the underlying problem. The United States continued to run large trade deficits.

In May 1971, West Germany announced that it would no longer sell German marks for U.S. dollars. The Germans were frustrated that the United States was refusing to redeem the dollars for gold, as contemplated at Bretton Woods. In the following three months, the U.S. dollar dropped 7.5% against the Deutschmark.

Meanwhile, France continued to convert its dollars to gold. In August 1971, the new French president, Georges Pompidou, sent a warship to New York to retrieve the additional gold.

Things were starting to fall apart, from an American perspective. By August 15, the United States had only 10,000 metric tons of gold remaining in the U.S. reserves. This was less than half of the peak amount.

On August 15, 1971, President Nixon announced that the United States would no longer redeem dollars for gold. The United States was leaving the gold standard, and "closing the gold window." Nixon also announced a 90-day freeze on wages and prices, and a 10% surcharge on imported goods.

This event became known as the "Nixon shock." The Nixon shock led to a floating rate exchange system, in which the value of currencies would be theoretically determined by supply and demand, for each nation's currency.

After the Nixon shock, the value of the U.S. dollar declined by approximately one-third. Since the dollar was no longer convertible to gold, other nations were not inclined to hold the currency. The markets began to speculate against the dollar.

The commodity markets, in particular, were unhappy. Previously, the Middle East oil producers had been willing to accept U.S. dollars because dollars were convertible to gold. Now, those dollars were suddenly worth 30% less.

In September 1971, the Organization of Petroleum Exporting Nations, known as OPEC, issued a joint communiqué stating that from then on, they would price oil in terms of a fixed amount of gold. The price of oil quickly rose 50%, in U.S. dollar terms – from $2.00 a barrel in 1971 to $3.00 in 1973.

OPEC's decision to price oil according to the price of gold threatened America's access to Middle East oil. In 1971, the United States imported 4.4 million barrels of oil per day, approximately 35% of total domestic oil consumption. Eighty percent of this oil came from the Middle East.

Western Europe, sensing blood in the waters, tried to get a piece of the action. In 1973, Germany proposed pricing oil in German marks. Germany's proposal was a threat to American access to Middle Eastern oil. If oil was priced in German marks, the United States would be forced to trade goods to Germany, to obtain the necessary currency to purchase oil. The German proposal was not successful.

Meanwhile, events in the Middle East were spinning out of control.

On October 6, 1973, Egypt and Syria attacked Israel's forces in the Sinai Peninsula and the Golan Heights. The United States responded by rushing aid to Israel.

On October 17, 1973, OPEC announced that it would not sell oil to the United States at all, in retaliation for America's support of Israel in the war. The embargo caused an upward spiral in oil prices. The price of oil quadrupled, rising from $3 a barrel, in early 1973, to nearly $12 a barrel later in the year. This led to a significant increase in the price of gasoline in the United States.

Triffin returns to Europe.

In 1977, economist Robert Triffin retired from Yale University, and returned to his native Belgium. Triffin accepted a visiting professorship at the University of Louvain, and became involved in European policy. He played a leading role in the creation of Europe's common currency, the euro.

Toward the end of his life, Triffin continued to brood about the future of the U.S. dollar. He wondered whether America's unrestrained printing would eventually lead to a dollar collapse. As he approached death, Triffin discussed the issue with friends. He said: "What will happen? I shall very soon find out."

Triffin died in Belgium in February 1993, a few months after the Maastricht Treaty paved the way for the creation of the euro.

CHAPTER 5

The New Gold Standard – the Petrodollar

In 1974, President Nixon was struggling to deal with the aftereffects of the Arab oil embargo. Nixon wanted a reliable supply of foreign oil, preferably priced in U.S. dollars.

The problem for Nixon was that much of the Middle East's oil was still priced in British pounds. This was due to how the oil fields were set up.

After World War I, Britain gained political control over much of the modern Middle East. Britain colonized Iraq, Palestine, Jordan, Kuwait, Bahrain, Qatar, the United Arab Emirates, and Oman. Britain also obtained a protectorate over Saudi Arabia.

During the 1920s, Britain developed the oil industry in many of these countries. Thus, Britain controlled some of the most productive oil fields on the planet.

In the early 1970s, this legacy of colonialism was unwinding.

Due to U.S. pressure, Britain was slowly withdrawing from its former colonies. Britain granted independence to Iraq and Saudi Arabia as early as 1932. Other nations, such as Bahrain, Qatar, and the

United Arab Emirates, did not gain their independence from Britain until 1971.

In the early 1970s, Saudi Arabia, Nigeria and Kuwait continued to price all or a portion of their oil exports in British pounds, also known as sterling.

Nixon's effort to price oil in U.S. dollars benefitted from a shift in the world's primary reserve currency, from pounds to the U.S. dollar.

In the mid-1960s, sterling still made up over 20% of global foreign exchange reserves. Some former British colonies continued to hold over 50% of their reserves in British pounds.

As Britain relinquished control over its former colonies, the world economy required fewer and fewer pounds. This caused the value of the currency to drop. In November 1967, Britain devalued the pound by 14.3%. Thus, by the early 1970s, the Middle East was open to using a stronger currency for pricing oil.

Nixon asked his Secretary of State, Henry Kissinger, to deal with the problem.

In July 1974, Kissinger flew to Saudi Arabia, to discuss pricing oil exclusively in U.S. dollars. Kissinger was accompanied by the new U.S. Treasury secretary, William Simon. Simon had previously run the Treasury bond desk at Salomon Brothers, in New York.

In secret negotiations, Kissinger offered to provide military support for Saudi Arabia, if Saudi Arabia agreed to price oil only in U.S. dollars. Kissinger and Simon also asked the Saudis to invest their dollar proceeds from oil in the United States, in Treasury bonds. Simon argued that U.S. bonds were the safest in the world.

The Saudis agreed to the deal, provided that their investment in U.S. Treasury bonds would be kept secret. The Saudis did not want to be publicly associated with the United States, so soon after the Arab oil boycott. Kissinger had no objection to keeping the investment secret.

On December 12, 1974, Saudi Arabia announced that it would no longer accept British pounds in return for oil. Until that date, about 25% of Saudi Arabia's payments for oil had been made in pounds, with the balance mostly in dollars. Now, Saudi Arabia signaled to the markets that it was only willing to accept United States dollars. Other oil producers in the Middle East followed suit, and soon accepted only U.S. dollars for oil.

After the Saudi decision, buyers of oil were forced to sell British pounds, and purchase United States dollars, to pay for oil. This placed pressure on the British pound, and served to bolster the value of the dollar. The New York Times described the event as follows:

> Leading bankers have been reporting for months that the major source of strength for sterling was Arab support, reflecting the heavy flow of oil funds. The loss of a significant part of that support is being viewed as a negative factor in sterling's value. Heavy selling of pounds swept through the exchange markets, and sterling closed with losses of varying sizes against the United States dollar, the French franc, the Swiss franc, the West German mark and most other major currencies.

The Saudi decision exacerbated a balance of payments crisis in Britain. By 1975, inflation in Britain was running 25%, leading to yet another run on pounds sterling. Between 1975 and 1977, the pound lost 40% of its value against the dollar.

Britain's pain was America's gain. Saudi Arabia's commitment to sell oil only for United States dollars provided support for the dollar. Now, instead of being backed by gold, the U.S. dollar was backed by oil, which was as good as gold.

The Middle East oil producers were soon flooded with U.S. dollars, which Americans used to purchase oil by the tanker load. Meanwhile, Saudi dollars flowed back to the United States, for investments in Treasury bonds and American stocks. Their investments became known as petrodollar recycling.

The petrodollar arrangement allowed the United States to print more dollars, and distribute the dollars throughout the world economy. Below is a chart of the federal budget deficit, between 1959 and 1985.

Table 5.1

United States Federal Budget Deficit

Fiscal Year	Deficit ($ billions)	Debt to GDP Ratio
1959	$13	2.5%
1960	$(1)	(0.1%)
1961	$3	0.6%
1962	$7	1.2%
1963	$5	0.7%
1964	$6	0.9%
1965	$1	0.2%
1966	$4	0.5%
1967	$9	1.0%
1968	$25	2.7%
1969	($3)	(0.3%)
1970	$3	0.3%
1971	$23	2.0%
1972	$23	1.8%
1973	$15	1.0%
1974	$6	0.4%
1975	$53	3.2%
1976	$74	3.9%
1977	$54	2.6%
1978	$59	2.5%

1979	$41	1.6%
1980	$74	2.6%
1981	$79	2.5%
1982	$128	3.8%
1983	$208	5.7%
1984	$185	4.6%
1985	$212	4.9%

After the petrodollar deal with Saudi Arabia in 1974, federal debt levels exploded. In 1975, the federal budget deficit tripled from an average of 1% of the United States economy to 3%, in a single year. In the early 1980s, the federal budget deficit became even larger – increasing to an average of 5% of GDP by the middle of the decade.

This spending put pressure on the value of the dollar. Below is a chart of the value of the dollar, vis-à-vis other major currencies.

Table 5.2

Dollar Index Value

Date	Dollar Index Value
4/1/1973	100.376
6/1/1973	97.483
9/1/1973	95.849
12/1/1973	98.292
3/1/1974	95.777
6/1/1974	94.423
9/1/1974	96.492
12/1/1974	94.697
3/1/1975	92.289
6/1/1975	92.665

Date	Value
9/1/1975	96.557
12/1/1975	96.352
3/1/1976	94.505
6/1/1976	94.559
9/1/1976	94.378
12/1/1976	94.446
3/1/1977	94.278
6/1/1977	93.66
9/1/1977	92.708
12/1/1977	89.705
3/1/1978	88.556
6/1/1978	88.79
9/1/1978	85.619
12/1/1978	86.23
3/1/1979	87.28
6/1/1979	89.457
9/1/1979	88.291
12/1/1979	89.588
3/1/1980	92.483
6/1/1980	88.923
9/1/1980	88.136
12/1/1980	90.621
3/1/1981	92.302
6/1/1981	98.347
9/1/1981	99.947
12/1/1981	97.197
3/1/1982	103.216

6/1/1982	106.916
9/1/1982	110.839
12/1/1982	107.047
3/1/1983	107.724
6/1/1983	110.775
9/1/1983	113.237
12/1/1983	113.845
3/1/1984	112.448
6/1/1984	116.2
9/1/1984	122.188
12/1/1984	123.401
3/1/1985	128.437

After Nixon's decision to close the gold window, foreign central banks reduced their exposure to the dollar. In 1970, foreign central banks held approximately 85% of their reserves in U.S. dollars. By 1978, they held only 58% of their reserves in dollars.

As central banks dumped dollars, the value of the dollar fell. From September 1977 to October 1978, the dollar fell 40% against the Japanese yen, 35% against the Swiss franc, and 13% against the deutsche mark. On a trade-weighted basis, the dollar declined by 19%, in a little over a year.

On November 1, 1978, U.S. President Jimmy Carter announced that the United States would intervene in currency markets to support the value of the dollar. The United States would do so, in coordination with officials from West Germany, Japan and Switzerland. To implement the plant, the United States marshalled a $30 billion fund consisting of Japanese yen, deutsche marks, and Swiss francs to support the dollar. The fund would be equal to about $150 billion in 2025 dollars.

By the end of 1978, the value of the dollar stabilized in currency markets, eliminating the crisis. Central banks began to purchase dollars, bringing the dollar to about 60% of foreign currency reserves by 1980.

Meanwhile, the petrodollar deal began to kick into full gear. By 1980, the dollar began to strengthen, as demand for oil increased and countries paid in U.S. dollars.

By 1980, other commodity producers priced their goods in U.S. dollars, as well. This included wheat, timber, copper, iron ore, and uranium. All of this trade added support for the value of the dollar in world currency markets.

As commodity markets shifted to the dollar, the United States found that it could run larger and larger trade deficits. If a commodity was priced in U.S. dollars, the United States got the commodity for free, because America could simply print dollars.

However, other countries on the planet were at a disadvantage to the United States. Every other country on the planet had to acquire dollars to purchase oil, or other commodities. This meant that they had to sell goods or services to the United States to get dollars. If a county did not have dollars, then that country did not have the means to operate a modern economy, which requires oil.

In 1980, the value of the dollar began to soar. Between October 1978 and March 1985, the value of the U.S. dollar index rose from 84 to 128 – an increase of 52%.

The petrodollar – by the numbers.

It is impossible to understate the importance of the petrodollar arrangement to American prosperity. For example, consider the world oil market. As of 2025, world oil production is approximately 105 million barrels of oil per day.

Let's assume that 80% of the world's oil is sold for dollars. That would be equal to 84 million barrels of oil per day. If the average price of oil is $65 dollars for a barrel, then those 84 million barrels of oil would cost 5.5 billion U.S. dollars per day. That is artificial demand for $5.5 billion per day.

If we multiply that number by 365 days per year, we find that 80% of the world's oil market creates artificial demand for $2 trillion U.S. dollars every year.

That's a lot of demand for U.S. dollars. And that's only 80% of the world's oil market. That number does not include all of the grains, timber, copper, iron ore, gold and uranium that are also sold in U.S. dollars.

Now, let's put $2 trillion in perspective. In 2024, the total value of U.S. exports of goods and services – coming from the United States – totaled $3.2 trillion dollars. In other words, 80% of the world's oil market – priced in U.S. dollars – creates artificial demand for the dollar equal to two-thirds of U.S. exports. The numbers are as follows:

Table 5.3

Demand for U.S. Dollars

Asset Category	Dollar Amount	Percent of U.S. GDP
Domestic U.S. exports	$3.2 trillion	61.5%
80% of world oil market	$2.0 trillion	38.5%
Total demand for dollars	$5.2 trillion	100.0%

To put it another way, nearly half of the demand for the dollar is artificial, because a large portion of world trade is done in dollars.

If the world's oil markets were to reject the U.S. dollar – and price oil in a currency other than the U.S. dollar – as we saw in December 1971 – then we can anticipate that the value of the U.S. dollar will fall by approximately 50%, against other major world currencies.

The drop could be larger, because other commodity markets, which currently price in dollars, would also likely reject the U.S. dollar. This would include the markets for copper, iron ore, wheat, timber and gold. It is possible that the dollar could drop by as much as 80%, if the world were to simultaneously reject the U.S. dollar, and trade most commodities in a different currency.

This artificial demand for the dollar has been a bonanza for the United States. Goods from all over the planet flow to the United States from countries seeking dollars. America receives autos and electronics from Japan; flat screen televisions from South Korea; manufactured goods from China; produce from Latin America; and car parts from Canada and Mexico. Virtually all of these goods are priced in U.S. dollars, which the United States is able to print at no cost.

However, the petrodollar arrangement poses a grave threat to the future of the United States. As we have seen, the ability to get free goods – by printing U.S. dollars – has made the United States weak. Large amounts of American manufacturing have shifted overseas, leaving American productive capacity weak.

In addition, the United States is using a currency that could potentially collapse in value. Economist Robert Triffin predicted this in 1960. His thesis can be stated as follows:

> When a national currency is used for the world's primary reserve currency, that currency will be overprinted leading to a loss in confidence.

Thus, we can expect that the world will eventually reject the U.S. dollar. The decline could happen gradually over time – or it could happen suddenly, as occurred in December 1971.

If the world's oil markets were to shift to an alternative currency in a sudden manner, then the value of the U.S. dollar could implode, plunging the United States into poverty overnight.

Let's consider how the petrodollar arrangement has affected the United States economy, since 1980.

De-industrialization begins.

There is a proverb that says, "rough winds make strong timber."

It means that adversity tends to build character, either in a person or a tree.

The same holds true for an economy. If you give 330 million people – i.e. the size of the United States – free access to oil and imported goods for fifty years, those people are going to get lazy. They will stop doing things for themselves. They will import everything they need, because the inputs to their economy are, essentially, free.

The United States has benefitted from a similar arrangement since 1974. Since oil is priced in U.S. dollars, the United States can import oil at essentially no cost to the population of our country.

Since 1980, the U.S. economy has atrophied as a result of the petrodollar monopoly. The United States has grown weak, both militarily and economically. The petrodollar has made it too expensive to manufacture many goods in the United States. As a result, entire communities have been wiped out. For example, let's take a closer look at the steel industry in the United States.

United States production of iron and steel peaked in 1973 – the year before our country acquired the petrodollar monopoly. In 1973, the United States produced 229 million metric tons of iron and steel.

After the deal with Saudi Arabia, United States production of iron and steel dropped dramatically. Production fell approximately 50% in just three years, between 1979 to 1982. By 1982, the United States produced only 107 million tons of iron and steel – less than half of its production a decade earlier.

These numbers had a dramatic impact on employment in the steel industry. In 1970, over 300,000 people were employed in the steel industry in Pittsburgh alone. In just two years -- 1981 and

1982 -- Pittsburgh's steel mills laid off 153,000 workers. That was approximately half of the steel-producing workforce.

By 1983, the unemployment rate in Pittsburgh hit 18%, with 212,000 people in the area out of work. To the west of Pittsburgh, in Beaver County, the unemployment rate rose to 27% -- a level not seen since the Great Depression. To the east, Jonestown was not working either, with an unemployment rate of 23%.

Many of us are familiar with Billy Joel's song, Allentown. In that song, Billy Joel sang of the difficulty of the Pennsylvania economy in the early 1980s:

> Well, we're living here in Allentown
> And they're closing all the factories down
> Out in Bethlehem, they're killing time
> Filling out forms, standing in line

The worst was yet to come. In 1982, the mills were still in place.

In 1984, the mills started to close permanently. In that year, the Aliquippa Works, located west of Pittsburgh along the Ohio River, permanently closed its doors. Aliquippa was a huge mill that formerly employed 17,000 workers. That same year, U.S. Steel closed the Duquesne Works, located to the east of Pittsburgh. The Duquesne Works had been one of Andrew Carnegie's three big mills, and had been in operation for more than a century.

In 1985, Jones & Laughlin closed its massive plant on the south side of Pittsburgh. Then the heaviest blow of all fell. The following year, U.S. Steel permanently closed the Homestead Works, formerly the largest steel mill in the world. Much of the equipment was so massive that it literally had to be blown up with dynamite. Residents in the surrounding communities heard the explosions in their former steel plant for over a year. In 1987, two other companies, National Tube and American Bridge, closed their plants in Ambridge.

By the end of the 1980s, over 75% of the steel production in the Pittsburgh area was gone. The percentage of Pittsburgh's population working in manufacturing fell from 28% in 1970 to only 10% in 2000.

The mill closings were an economic catastrophe for the Pittsburgh region. Former steelworkers spread out across the United States, looking for work. During the 1980s, 200,000 people left the Pittsburgh region. During the 1990s, another 100,000 people moved out of the area. The Pittsburgh region lost 30% of its population.

By 2000, nearly 400,000 people had left the region. "Steeler bars," which focused on the Pittsburgh Steelers football team sprung up all over the United States, marking the landing sites of the diaspora.

Pittsburgh's young population was especially affected by the plant closures, since they were the first to be laid off. They fled the region, making Allegheny County, Pennsylvania one of the oldest counties in the United States, demographically.

The former steel workers went on to new lives, in a vastly-different United States. Rather than working near blast furnaces in dirty steel mills, they went on to cleaner jobs in America's new service economy. They became car salesmen, selling cars that were increasingly imported. They built houses in the south of the United States. They sold insurance, became lawyers, or were involved in the tourism industry.

At first glance, their lives were vastly improved. There were fewer workplace accidents. Food and imported goods flowed into our country from every corner of the planet. No one had to work hard, because, increasingly, the dirty work was done overseas. Rather than make steel in the United States, the hot work was done in places such as Shanghai, China; Russia; South Korea; Eastern Europe; or India.

The change in the U.S. economy was propelled by the petrodollar monopoly, set up by Nixon and Kissinger fifteen years earlier. No one understood that that monopoly on the sale of oil trade is temporary. Like all restraints on trade, the monopoly will not last forever. When the monopoly is lost, the bonanza generated by the oil-backed dollars will cease.

Let's take a closer look at what the future of the United States could look like.

Pittsburgh – harbinger of economic collapse.

I lived in Pittsburgh for five years, between May 2000 and June 2005. This was approximately twenty years after the mills closed, scattering the steel workers to the wind.

What I saw astonished me. It was like living in a time machine. No one had invested in Pittsburgh since the late 1960s. The place was a ruin, consisting of worn out and torn up infrastructure. Everywhere, I saw old buildings in disrepair, abandoned houses, and boarded-up store fronts. Much of the housing stock consisted of red brick buildings from the 1920s, built during the heyday of America's steel production. Signage on some of the shops dated from the mid-1960s, as no one was interested in the Pittsburgh market.

Many of the old mill towns, located along the Ohio, Allegheny and Monongahela Rivers, had lost well over half of their populations. Homestead, Pennsylvania had lost 85% of its population, as of 2000. Ambridge -- the former home of American Bridge Company -- lost 61% of its population. McKees Rocks lost 67% of its population. McKeesport – the site of one of the Nixon-Kennedy debates in 1960 – lost nearly two-thirds of its population. Braddock – the site of one of Andrew Carnegie's mills since 1872 -- lost an astonishing 86% of its population.

These abandoned mill towns fascinated me. They weren't filled with bars, serving martinis to young professionals. And they were no longer selling beer to steel workers. Instead, these worn-out mill towns were a graphic lesson of what happens when you remove industry from an area. You get ghost towns, poverty, drug addiction and crime.

In Duquesne, Pennsylvania, I explored a 100-year-old abandoned Catholic church. It still had its floor and roof. However, the windows and seats had been removed. The building was in a state of ruin, and would soon collapse.

In Homestead, I explored the site of Andrew Carnegie's first public library. The library and its swimming pool remained open. However, the facility and the surrounding community had fallen on hard times. An old wooden display case showed loving cup trophies from long-forgotten wresting and swimming events in the 1940s.

Allegheny County's poverty rate skyrocketed after the mill closings in the 1980s. Consider for example, the former mill town of Braddock, Pennsylvania. As of 2009, 58% of Braddock had an income below the poverty level, compared to 16% for the state of Pennsylvania. Today, Braddock is the poorest town in Allegheny County. According to John Fetterman, the former mayor of Braddock, the poverty rate in Braddock is three times the national average. The high rates of poverty in the Monongahela River Valley have fostered rampant drug-abuse, which has increased crime rates.

The World War II generation fights back.

The destruction of Pittsburgh was distressing for America's leaders. America's leaders of 1980 remembered the Great Depression, and were determined to do what they could to avoid a recurrence of that event.

Let's go back to the Great Depression, to understand their thinking.

On October 24, 1929 – fifty years before the collapse of Pittsburgh – the Dow Jones average fell 21%. That day became known as "Black Thursday." The following Monday, the market declined another 13%. The next day, the market fell an additional 12%.

By mid-November 1932, stocks had lost half of their value. By the summer of 1933, the market was down 89%. Many people lost everything.

The market collapse caused a major depression in the United States. Between 1929 and 1932, unemployment rose 400%. By 1932, 25% of the nation's families did not have an employed wage earner. Twelve million people were out of work, in a much smaller population.

Those who were lucky enough to keep a job experienced falling wages, and reduced work hours. Ninety percent of employers were forced to cut pay. By 1933, average wages were down 40%. By 1932, three-quarters of all workers in the United States were working part-time, averaging just two-thirds of a normal week.

Millions of families lost their homes. People were forced to live wherever they could find shelter. In Pennsylvania, groups of families gathered in one-room shacks, and lived on wild weeds. In Arkansas, families lived in caves. In Oakland, California, some families lived in sewer pipes. Others sought refuge in railroad boxcars. In 1931 alone, the Southern Pacific Railroad removed 683,000 persons from its trains.

The African American community was particularly hard-hit. In 1930, 70% of Charleston's black population and 75% of Memphis's black community were unemployed.

Then, as if things weren't bad enough, the rain stopped.

Between 1930 and 1940, the United States experienced a severe drought in the lower Great Plains. The drought extended from the Appalachian mountains, in the east, to the Rocky mountains, in the west. This region – affecting some thirty states – became known as the "Dust Bowl."

Large numbers of families lost their farms due to the drought. In 1936, losses reached the equivalent of half a billion dollars per day, in today's dollars.

The drought caused large-scale migration in the United States. About 2.5 million people fled the southern Great Plains during the 1930s. These people primarily moved to California, in search of work and a better life. The refugees gathered in shanty towns, on the edge of small communities in California. Conditions in the shanty towns were appalling, and hunger was widespread.

In his book, The Grapes of Wrath, John Steinbeck described the plight of the refugees. According to Steinbeck, the refugees were forced to live on a diet consisting of little more than potatoes and fried dough. People were willing to work an entire day in the California fields, simply to buy a spoonful of flour, and some cooking oil. The refugees, and millions of unemployed people, could not afford meat, milk and fresh vegetables.

Needless to say, the refugees were not welcome. The California police harassed the new arrivals, and sometimes burned the shanty towns. There was already little work in California. Conditions were made worse, by the sudden arrival of hundreds of thousands – and then millions – of new people seeking work.

And yes, people died from malnutrition. It is estimated that tens of thousands of people died in the United States from lack of proper food, during the 1930s.

When I grew up, I heard stories about life in the United States during the 1930s. My father, Albert Schuchardt, was born in 1928. He was one of eight children that grew up in a small wooden house on the edge of Madison, Wisconsin. Our nation's standard of living was much lower at that time. The family raised chickens, for eggs and meat. The family did not have running water. These experiences were typical of life in the United States during those years.

America's leaders of 1980 remembered these images. They understood that America was not always rich. They understood that wealth has to be created, and saved for a rainy day. They knew that if the factories were closed, then people went hungry.

Stockpiling

These experiences led the World War II generation to view the economy differently than today's generation of leaders. For example, our parents' generation stockpiled everything.

In 1946, Congress directed the Army and Navy to identify strategic materials critical to the nation's defense, and to establish stockpiles of those materials. The Pentagon began to gather large quantities of aluminum, chromium, cobalt, diamonds, manganese, platinum, tin, tungsten and zinc. These were stored at stockpiles located on army bases around the United States.

By December 1952, the United States had amassed a stockpile worth $4.02 billion, or $45 billion in today's dollars. Imports of materials were permitted only from Canada and Mexico.

In 1962, President Kennedy was astonished to find that the United States had accumulated $7.7 billion worth of materials, an amount equal to $75.7 billion in today's dollars. Economists estimated that this was nearly double the amount required for America's wartime needs.

Strategic Grain Reserve

The World War II generation also stockpiled grains.

The idea of a grain reserve is as old as the Bible itself. In the book of Exodus, the Bible tells how the Pharoah in Egypt stored one-fifth of the harvest for each of seven years, in anticipation of seven years of drought. The United States used to do the same thing, due to the hunger experienced during the Great Depression.

In the 1950s and 1960s, the federal government bought corn and wheat, and held them in government warehouses. In 1960, the United States held over 2 billion bushels of corn and wheat in reserves. This was equal to approximately two years of domestic consumption. Needless to say, the World War II generation slept well at night.

However, the cost of storing the grain was high. In the 1970s, Congress passed a law to pay farmers to store the grain. The program continued in place until the 1990s.

Strategic Petroleum Reserve.

With the oil crisis of the early 1970s, the World War II generation began to stockpile crude oil. In 1975, Congress created a Strategic Petroleum Reserve to mitigate the impact of a future crisis involving America's oil supply.

The reserve they created is, in theory, the largest petroleum reserve in the world. It can hold up to 714 million barrels of crude oil in underground caverns located in Louisiana and Texas.

By 1982, the reserve held almost 300 million barrels of oil. Throughout the 1980s, the United States continued to add oil to reserve on a regular basis. By 1990, the reserve held approximately 600 million barrels of oil. The reserve then remained stable at about that level until the early 2000s.

Civil Defense Preparation

The World War II generation prepared for everything, including a possible nuclear war. In 1961, the Kennedy Administration started a civil defense program that sought to shelter two-thirds of the United States population from radiation, in the event of a nuclear war. The government marked over 14,000 locations with black and yellow fallout shelter signs. The government stockpiled these locations with emergency supplies, consisting of radiological meters, food supplies, water, and sanitation kits.

While well-meaning, the program was not long-lasting. Many of the shelters were located in urban centers, that would likely be destroyed by blast effects, in the event of a war. The program was abandoned in 1971. Later in the decade, the Carter administration proposed a new civil defense program intended to move two-thirds of the population to rural areas, in the event of a war. However, that program was not carried out, due to feasibility concerns.

1985 -- The Plaza Accord

The above events describe the mindset of America's leaders in the early to mid-1980s. These leaders understood the importance of industry, and the connection of industry to the well-being of the population.

When the Pittsburgh economy collapsed in the early 1980s, the World War II generation was determined to protect American manufacturing, and jobs.

Many believed that Pittsburgh's collapse was caused by the high dollar, and competition from imported steel. Other industries felt threatened.

In the early-1980s, an alliance of manufacturers and farmers began to lobby the federal government for protection from foreign competition. The alliance included grain exporters, the auto industry, and high-tech companies, such as IBM and Motorola. These companies wanted to protect their exports. If the dollar became too expensive, vis-à-vis other competing currencies, then the United States could not sell products overseas.

In 1985, Congress considered passing protectionist laws. To avoid these laws, the Reagan administration opted to reduce the value of the dollar, through intervention in the currency markets.

On September 22, 1985, the United States entered into an agreement with Britain, France, West Germany and Japan to lower the value of the dollar, through currency purchases. The deal became known as the Plaza Accord, for the name of the New York hotel where the parties met.

The agreement was successful. Between March 1985 and May 1995, the U.S. dollar index fell from 128 to 84, a 35% decline. This reduction provided relief to American manufacturers and farmers.

However, the Plaza Accord did not deal with the fundamental problem with the U.S. economy. The problem was then – and still is – an overvalued dollar, caused by the petrodollar arrangement with the Middle East.

Protection of the auto industry.

The World War II generation sought to protect the U.S. economy in other ways. Foreign competition in the auto industry was a significant concern.

Germany and Japan were the first countries to export cars to the United States. Germany's Volkswagen started selling cars in the United

States in 1949. Japanese competition started in 1957, when Toyota began to export cars to our country.

Sales were initially slow. In the 1950s, Americans viewed Germany and Japan with suspicion, and some hostility, due to the war. Japanese products, in particular, were viewed as inferior to those made in the United States. However, both Volkswagen and Toyota soon upgraded their quality.

In 1958, Toyota sold 285 sedans in the United States. By 1966, the company was selling over 20,000 cars annually in America. Only four years later, in 1970, Toyota had increased this number to 216,000 vehicles – a tenfold increase in sales.

In 1965, 5% of all cars sold in the United States were imported. By 1971, this number had increased to nearly 16%. The top exporters of vehicles to the United States were Toyota, Volkswagen and the Japanese company, Datsun.

After the fuel crisis of 1973 and 1974, Americans flocked to the smaller, fuel-efficient cars made by the Germans and Japanese. By 1975, foreign car sales in the United States were close to one million units, accounting for nearly 20% of all new cars sold in the United States.

In the next five years, sales of imported cars doubled in the United States. In 1980, foreign car makers sold 2.4 million vehicles in the United States – over a quarter of the new car market.

At this point, America's leaders had had enough. Domestic car manufacturers were not keeping up on quality or price. Factories were closing, and American jobs were being lost to Japan and Germany.

At that time, the petrodollar was not understood. Congress did not understand that Ford, GM and Chrysler could not compete because the U.S. currency was artificially too high.

In 1981, the United States negotiated a "voluntary export restraint" agreement with Japan, concerning automobiles. The agreement limited the number of cars that Japan could export to the U.S. to 1.68 million units per year. The United States did not impose any sort of export restraint – or "VER agreement" – on the German car makers.

Japan responded to the 1981 VER agreement by setting up production in the United States. By 1985, Japan's three largest Japanese auto manufacturers had all opened factories in the United States. These facilities were located primarily in the southern states. This was due to incentives offered by state governments, the weakness of unions in the south, and a cheaper labor pool.

Efforts to avoid currency manipulation.

The World War II generation also took steps to prevent countries from manipulating the value of their currency, to gain an advantage against the United States.

The value of a country's currency makes a big difference in the competitiveness of that country. For example, consider a Japanese car that sold for $10,000 in 1980. If Japan were to reduce its currency – the yen – by 15% versus the dollar, then the cost of that car in the United States would be 15% lower. Instead of costing $10,000, the car would have sticker price of only $8,500. (This is assuming that there are no other import duties on the car.) The lower currency acts as a subsidy on Japan's car sales in the United States.

Similarly, the lower currency serves as a de facto Japanese tax on America's exports to Japan. Cars made in the United States would be more expensive in Japan. People in Japan, purchasing with yen, would be able to purchase 15% fewer dollars with the same amount of yen. A car that would normally sell for $10,000 in Japan would be 15% more expensive in yen terms, costing a Japanese buyer the equivalent of $11,500.

In the 1980s, countries learned to manipulate their currencies in a variety of ways. Some countries – such as Japan and Switzerland – used negative interest rates. Instead of paying interest on money deposited in Japan and Switzerland, these countries charged third parties a small "negative interest rate" to keep money in their currency. This discouraged foreigners from holding large amounts of Japanese yen or Swiss francs, and thus helped to keep the value of the currency low.

Other countries, such as China, controlled the exchange rate by simply setting the exchange rate at a value below the market value for the currency. This enabled China to keep its manufacturing costs below that of competing nations.

Throughout the 1980s, it became increasingly clear that some countries were manipulating their currencies, to gain an advantage in international trade. The Plaza Accord was one effort to deal with this problem. However, Congress felt that the problem had not been completely solved.

In 1988, Congress passed the Omnibus Trade and Competitiveness Act. The law requires the U.S. Treasury Secretary to monitor the currencies of America's major trading partners. The Treasury Secretary is required to provide a regular report to Congress, as to whether any country is intentionally manipulating the value of its currency, to obtain an unfair advantage in trade.

If a country is found to be manipulating its currency, then the law requires the Treasury Department to negotiate with that country, to adjust the exchange rate to a fairer value.

Following the passage of the law, the process of identifying trade delinquents became a political football. Companies importing goods into the United States wanted the currency of their supplier nations to be cheap. They therefore wanted no designation of "trade manipulation" on their trading partners.

Between 1988 and 1994, the federal government – run by the World War II generation – enforced the law. During those years, the United States identified three countries as currency-manipulators under the law. These were South Korea in 1988, Taiwan in 1988 and 1992, and China from 1992 to 1994.

However, things began to change in the early 1990s, when a new generation of leaders obtained political power.

1992 -- the turning point in American politics

The year 1992 was a turning point in recent United States politics. That year, the American people had to choose between two different generations of leaders.

The Republican candidate, George H.W. Bush, was born in 1924.

Bush was a member of the World War II generation. On his eighteenth birthday, in 1942, Bush enlisted in the U.S. Navy, where he served as an aviator. He flew his first combat mission in 1944, when he bombed Wake Island. Later that year, the Japanese shot down Bush's plane. Bush survived, and was rescued by an American naval ship. Bush later became a successful businessman and ran for Congress.

Bush's opponent, Arkansas governor Bill Clinton, represented a new generation in American leaders. Clinton was born in 1946 -- after the conclusion of the Second World War.

Clinton was a member of the "Baby Boom generation," born between the years 1946 and 1964. As a member of this generation, Clinton had no memory of the Great Depression or World War II.

Clinton's earliest memories, from perhaps 1950, would have been of the growing prosperity in the United States following the war.

In the early 1950s, the U.S. economy boomed. The number of autos produced in the United States quadrupled in the decade between 1946 and 1955. As a child, Clinton would have remembered the typical images of the 1950s – families acquiring their first car; families moving to new homes in the suburbs; telephones and televisions coming to every house in America; Elvis Presley; and ice cream at soda fountains.

Between 1950 and 1959, the U.S. economy grew by 37%. Growth accelerated during the 1960s. During the 1960s, the U.S. economy grew by an additional 53%, with average growth of about 5% each year.

Clinton's childhood was thus very different from that experienced by Bush. The economic conditions of the 1930s were the opposite of what Clinton experienced in the 1960s.

Clinton made different choices concerning military service, as well. Clinton turned 18 years old in August 1964 – a few months before President Johnson ramped up a bombing campaign in the Vietnam War. Clinton never served in that war. It has been alleged that Clinton used his connections in Washington, D.C. to avoid serving in the military.

Thus, Clinton and Bush came from different worlds, and had two different world-views.

There was a third candidate for president in 1992, as well. That candidate was businessman H. Ross Perot. Like Bush, Perot was a member of the World War II generation. Perot was born in 1930, in Texas. His first memories were likely of the poverty caused by the Depression.

As a young man, Perot served in the U.S. Navy. He later became a salesman for IBM. In 1962, Perot founded Electronic Data Systems (EDS), a data processing company. Twenty years later, in 1984, Perot sold EDS to General Motors for $2.4 billion. The sale made Perot one of the wealthiest people in our nation.

During the 1992 election, Perot expressed concerned about the U.S. federal budget deficit. Perot wanted the deficit lower.

Throughout the 1980s, the deficit continued to grow, as the politicians in the District of Columbia increased spending. By 1992, the deficit had reached 4.5% of GDP.

Table 5.3

United States Federal Deficit

Fiscal Year	Deficit ($ billions)	Debt Increase ($ billions)	Debt to GDP Ratio
1979	$41	$55	1.6%
1980	$74	$81	2.6%
1981	$79	$90	2.5%
1982	$128	$144	3.8%

1983	$208	$235	5.7%
1984	$185	$195	4.6%
1985	$212	$251	4.9%
1986	$221	$302	4.8%
1987	$150	$225	3.1%
1988	$155	$252	3.0%
1989	$153	$255	2.7%
1990	$221	$376	3.7%
1991	$269	$432	4.4%
1992	$290	$399	4.5%

During the 1992 campaign, Perot called for a balanced federal budget. Perot also famously opposed the North American Free Trade Agreement, often referred to as "NAFTA." The agreement was designed to make it easier for American companies to set up factories in Mexico or Canada. To do this, the agreement eliminated most tariffs between the United States, Mexico and Canada over a fifteen year period. The agreement set up special courts in Mexico, to consider disputes between American companies and Mexican property owners.

Perot argued that NAFTA would destroy the American industrial base, by shipping jobs and factories to Mexico. During a presidential debate in 1992, Perot argued that the agreement would create a great "sucking sound," as factories left the United States. He said:

> We have got to stop sending jobs overseas. It's pretty simple: If you're paying $12, $13, $14 an hour for factory workers and you can move your factory South of the border, pay a dollar an hour for labor, have no health care that's the most expensive single element in making a car have no environmental controls, no pollution controls and no retirement, and you don't care about anything but making money,

there will be a giant sucking sound going south.

> When [Mexico's] jobs come up from a dollar an hour to six dollars an hour, and ours go down to six dollars an hour . . . you've wrecked the country with these kinds of deals.

Perot called for "economic nationalism." By economic nationalism, he wanted an increased role of government in directing the economy, and for tariffs to protect the industrial base.

In June 1992, a Gallup poll showed Perot leading a three-way race against then-President Bush and Democratic nominee, Bill Clinton. However, Perot's poll numbers began to drop, as both parties attacked him in the media.

In July, Perot withdrew from the race, claiming that political opponents were harassing members of his family. Perot re-entered the race in early October. However, by that point, he had lost the lead, and was not viewed as a serious candidate by many.

In the end, Perot ended up splitting the vote, giving the contest to Clinton. The final vote was as follows:

Table 5.4

1992 United States Election

Candidate	Percentage of Vote
Bill Clinton	43.0%
George H.W. Bush	37.5%
Ross Perot	18.9%

Clinton won the election with 43% of the vote. Bush came in second with 37% of the vote, followed by Perot with nearly 19% of the vote.

On January 20, 1993, Clinton was sworn in as the 42nd President of the United States.

Clinton's inauguration was approximately fifty years after the end of the Second World War. The World War II generation was now in its 70s and 80s, and had lost power to a younger group of Americans. The new leaders, represented by Clinton and his successors, George W. Bush, Barrack Obama, and Joe Biden, were untested by economic adversity or a significant war. They would show an astonishing lack of judgment in their stewardship of the U.S. economy.

The baby boomers sell the crown jewels.

There's an old adage that says "shirtsleeves to shirtsleeves in three generations." It means that -- within a family -- wealth is created and destroyed in three generations. The first generation creates the wealth; the second generation conserves the wealth; and the third generation consumes the wealth. Statistically, the adage is true. Typically, 90% of a family's wealth is gone by the end of the third generation.

The cycle of wealth-creation and destruction is described in Pearl Buck's book, The Good Earth. In the book, Pearl Buck describes the life of a Chinese peasant in the 1920s. The peasant -- Wang Lung -- saves his money, and with great effort, purchases a small parcel of land. With additional effort, Wang Lung acquires a second parcel of property. Before long, he has employees working the land, and silver begins to flow in.

After a number of years, the former landlords in the area fell on hard times, and began to sell their land. Wang Lung starts buying their property, a parcel at a time. Eventually, Wang Lung purchases the mansion previously occupied by the former landlords, and sets up his family as the new "great house" in the area.

However, the story does not end there. Wang Lung always told his children, "No matter what happens, never sell the land. Never, ever sell the land." Wang Lung understood that wealth came from the land. At the end of the book, Wang Lung has grown old, and does not know that his children have started selling the land.

Pearl Buck's book could be a business school case study. Any first year business student will tell you that wealth is created by ownership of the means of production. Wealth is lost when one sells the machine tools. This is known as "eating one's seed corn." If you eat the seed corn, the business owner may feel wealthy for a short period of time. However, there will be grave problems in the future, because the harvest will be smaller.

After assuming power, in 1992, the Baby Boomers wasted no time in selling our nation's seed corn. They did this in a variety of ways.

North American Free Trade Agreement

The first thing the Baby Boomers did was push the machine tools out the door. Clinton did this by means of the North American Free Trade Agreement.

When Clinton announced his support for NAFTA, he claimed that the agreement would protect the common man in the United States. He said that the pact would increase U.S. exports to Mexico.

Others disagreed. Senator Howard Metzenbaum of Ohio predicted that the pact would cost 550,000 jobs over the next ten years in the United States. The Institute for International Economics estimated that the United States would lose 112,000 jobs in the first five years under the agreement. Many labor unions strongly opposed the deal.

Clinton spent much of 1993 lobbying to pass NAFTA. Finally, on November 20, 1993, Congress approved the bill.

It didn't take long for America's businesses to start moving jobs out of the United States. Foreign investment in Mexico tripled in the years after 1994.

- General Electric began to assemble all its gas ranges in Mexico.
- Thomson Consumer Electronics announced the closure of its factory in Bloomington, Indiana, and moved big-screen TV assembly to Mexico.

- Master Lock established a factory in Nogales, Mexico. The company eliminated over 1,000 union positions in Milwaukee.
- AT&T expanded production of answering machines at a $200 million plant in Guadalajara, Mexico. Corning Inc. entered into a $300 million joint venture with a Mexican glass manufacturing company, to make dishes, cooking utensils and silverware in Mexico, and sell them in the United States.
- Kemet, an electronics company, laid off 1,000 workers at a factory in Shelby, North Carolina, and transferred the plant to Monterrey, Mexico.

The auto and textile industries were particularly hard hit. Each industry lost hundreds of thousands of jobs.

Over the next twenty years, Mexico became the 4th largest auto exporter globally. Today, the Mexican auto industry employs over one million workers, in production hubs located around the country. These hubs make cars for General Motors, Ford, Stellantis, Volkswagen, Nissan, Mazda, Honda, BMW, Kia, Hyundai, and Audi.

Mexico is now the largest exporter of trucks and automotive parts to the United States. Mexico is also the second largest exporter of passenger cars to the U.S. market.

If you travel to the Mexican border, you will notice a steady stream of trucks moving north across the border, into the United States. Along the border, on the American side, you will find acres of refrigerated units, storing fruits and vegetables imported into the United States.

This physical traffic is the legacy of NAFTA. It represents a significant shift in the balance of trade between the United States and Mexico. In 1990, the United States had a trade surplus with Mexico of about $960 million, just under $1 billion. In 2024, the United States had a trade deficit with Mexico of approximately $172 billion. That is a negative shift of approximately 18-fold, or 18,000%. That can hardly be viewed as a gain to the United States.

Liquidation of Strategic Grain Reserve.

Clinton also liquidated America's strategic grain reserve. In May 1990, the United States still maintained a strategic grain reserve. Our nation stored about 800 million bushels of wheat and 1.3 billion bushels of corn. This was enough wheat to feed the country for nine months, and enough corn for two months.

Clinton eliminated these reserves. The 1996 Farm Bill repealed the grain stockpile program, which had been in place for half a century. As a result, the United States now has no strategic grain reserve, other than the grains which are already in the system.

Today, the United States relies upon a combination of existing stocks and annual production to meet domestic and international food needs. It is difficult to determine how much wheat and corn the United States has to feed its population. To estimate this number, economists look at a statistic called "carry out stocks." Carry out stocks refers to the amount of the prior year's crop that remains, when a new crop year begins. When we look at this number, the United States has between one month and six months of grain supplies, depending upon the particular grain.

Sale of the Strategic Petroleum Reserve.

Clinton also started drawing down the Strategic Petroleum Reserve (SPR) – only twenty years after the World War II generation created the program.

On April 30, 1996 – on the eve of the national presidential election – Clinton announced that the United States would sell 12 million barrels from the SPR, in an effort to lower oil prices in the election year. This was the first time that a president had used the reserve for political purposes.

The sale of oil did not materially affect prices. In subsequent years, politicians of both parties used this gimmick to try and gain votes. In

September 2000 – on the eve of the election between George W. Bush and Al Gore – Clinton ordered the release of 30 million more barrels of oil from the reserve.

After 2010, Congress began to sell the oil reserve, in earnest. Between 2017 and 2021, the U.S. Department of Energy sold at least 132 million barrels of oil from the SPR. This was about 18% of the reserve.

During the summer of 2022 – shortly before the mid-term elections – President Joe Biden ordered the U.S. Department of Energy to sell 260 million additional barrels of oil from the stockpile. Biden sold a portion of the oil to China, which allegedly used the oil to bolster its own oil reserve.

Biden's action reduced the SPR by about 40% from its level when he took office, in January 2021. By early 2023, the reserve had dropped to about half of its former level, or about 371.6 million barrels of oil. According to the Energy Information Administration, this was the lowest level since 1983.

Saudi Arabia's energy chief -- Prince Abdulaziz bin Salman -- warned the United States that it was foolish to sell its oil reserves. In a comment to the media, the prince said: "It is my profound duty to make clear to the world that losing emergency stocks may be painful in the months to come." The releases could lead to supply shortages in the future, according to the prince.

By July 2023, Congress had authorized the sale of more than half of the SPR. In that month, the reserve fell to about 346 million barrels, a 52% total reduction.

According to legislation already in place, the amount of oil in the reserve could fall to as little as 238 million barrels by 2028. This would be a 67% reduction of oil in the reserve since 2010.

Liquidation of National Defense Stockpiles.

President Clinton also sold off the National Defense Stockpiles. In 1992, Congress authorized the sale of substantially all of the nation's strategic mineral reserve. The reserve consisted of large amounts of cobalt, chromium, platinum, and manganese.

In 1952, the stockpile was worth $42 billion, in inflation-adjusted dollars. As of 2021, the stockpile was worth only $888 million. That is a 98% reduction in the National Defense Stockpile.

In 2008, the National Academy of Sciences questioned whether the United States was ready to fight a war. In a report prepared for the Department of Defense, the Academy noted that America's supply chains for critical materials appeared to be vulnerable.

The Academy noted that the Pentagon was increasingly dependent upon private industry, which imported most of its raw materials, on a just-in-time basis:

> There does not appear to be a strong relationship between stockpile policy and national security objectives; nor is there an understanding of global supply chain management practice. The . . . operation and future of the NDS have never been high on the agenda of the DoD leadership, nor do they seem to be now.

The Academy recommended that the United States take action to restore some of the defense stockpiles.

Sale of American Technology.

Trade secrets have long been viewed as sources of national wealth and power. For centuries, China closely guarded silk-making technology. China only permitted the export of finished silk items. It did not authorize the export of silkworms, or knowledge of how to weave silk.

China continues to follow this policy today, with modern technologies. The Wall Street Journal recently reported that China is assembling a list of its citizens involved in the production of rare earth elements. These citizens are not permitted to travel abroad. China does not want its trade secrets leaking out to the West.

America's third generation of wealth – represented by Presidents Clinton and Barack Obama – cared little about protecting American trade secrets. They were happy to sell American technology, together with the machine tools.

In 1998, President Clinton authorized U.S. companies to sell nuclear technology to China. This allowed American businesses to teach China how to build nuclear power plants. China used this technology to become a world leader in constructing nuclear plants around the world.

In 2009, President Barack Obama made a speech in Beijing. During that speech, Obama pledged U.S. government cooperation in transferring aerospace technology to China. China used this cooperation to develop its own version of Boeing's commercial jetliner. Today, China competes with Boeing and Airbus in the sale of this important technology.

In 2010, President Obama made a speech in Mexico City. During the speech, Obama boasted of making Mexico a world-class manufacturing country. He claimed that the United States had made Mexico an industry leader in making cars and flat screen televisions. Meanwhile, the United States produces few, if any, flat screen televisions.

The China shock.

America's "third generation" leaders cared nothing about enforcing the law against currency manipulation. They wanted the dollar as high as possible – and foreign currencies as low as possible – to maximize profits from imported goods.

China worked with America's leaders, and pegged the value of its currency as low as possible to the U.S. dollar. Below is a chart of the value of the Chinese yuan to the U.S. dollar, from 1981 to 2012:

Table 5.5
Exchange Rate -- Chinese Yuan to U.S. Dollar

Date	Yuan to the Dollar
January 1981	1.55
January 1982	1.77
January 1983	1.92
January 1984	2.05
January 1985	2.81
January 1986	3.21
January 1987	3.73
January 1990	4.73
January 1991	5.24
January 1992	5.46
January 1993	5.78
January 1994	8.72
January 1995	8.46
January 1996	8.34
January 2004	8.28
January 2006	8.07
January 2007	7.79
January 2008	7.24
January 2009	6.84
January 2011	6.60

January 2012   6.31

From the above chart, we can see that China changed its attitude about exchange rates, between 1981 and 1994.

When China first moved to a market economy, in 1981, China priced its currency at near par with the U.S. dollar. In other words, China would give foreigners just one and a half yuan for every dollar. This made doing business in China expensive.

During the 1980s, China relaxed its exchange rate. In January 1990, China was willing to sell 4.73 yuan for every dollar. This was a devaluation of 67% against the dollar.

In January 1994, China cut its exchange rate in half again, and was willing to pay 8.72 yuan for every dollar exchanged. This was a 54% reduction from 1990, and an 82% discount from 1981. At this price, Chinese goods became irresistible to the Fortune 500.

I visited China in April 1996, when the exchange rate was fixed at 8.34 yuan to the dollar. At that time, prices in China were astonishingly low, in dollar terms. During the visit, I stayed with two friends, who were teaching English at a teacher's college in Lishi, China. Each night, for a week, we went to a local restaurant, and ordered plates of Chinese food for the entire table. The food was spectacular. The cost of the feast, each night, for the three of us, was only $8 U.S. dollars. At that time, $8 would buy a sandwich in midtown Manhattan. Thus, prices were very low in China, at the exchange rate in effect in 1996.

Conditions in China, in 1996, were primitive compared to the United States. It had only been a few years since China abandoned socialism, and moved towards a market-oriented economy. Few people could afford cars, or even motorbikes. Most people traveled on bicycles.

There was little color in the country. Most people wore dark clothes, that did not draw attention to themselves. There were few billboards, or outdoor advertising. The buildings were often decades old, and made of bricks blackened by coal dust. About the only color I saw was the green top of outdoor pool tables, and an occasional Coca-Cola sign.

In 1996, China was just building modern infrastructure. The airport in Xi'an was brand new, but nearly empty. The same could be said about the country's highways. When my bus entered Beijing in April 1996, traffic was not a problem. The highway was new and uncongested. Only a few trucks were on the road, and few cars. Today, this same highway is jammed with vehicles of all sorts. It would be unimaginable to simply drive into the center of Beijing, without a delay.

In 1996, China had not yet modernized its train system. The train from Beijing to Shenzhen, in the south, near Hong Kong, took 36 hours. That was a day and half on a slow, creaking train. On the way south, I saw farmers plowing fields with water buffalo. Today, you can complete that same journey in less than eight hours – just one-fourth of the time of my trip thirty years ago.

In 1996, China was not yet a member of the club, for international trade. To be accepted by the West, China had to be a member of the World Trade Organization (WTO). Membership in the WTO meant that a country would benefit from low tariffs, known as the "most favorable nation" rate.

In the late 1990s, American businesses began clamoring to admit China into the WTO. They wanted to manufacture goods in China, and import them to the United States.

For several years, Congress hesitated, concerned about labor conditions in China. Finally, in 2001, the United States consented to China joining the WTO. The following year, the Bush administration granted China "most favorable nation" status. As a result, import duties for Chinese-made goods fell to the lowest possible level. China was in business.

After China's entry into the WTO, the United States experienced what economists call the "China Shock." The China Shock refers to a surge of imports from China, that occurred between 2000 and 2012. During this period, China's annual exports to the United States quadrupled, from $100 billion to $424 billion.

Factories in the United States closed by the tens of thousands, as businesses shipped their machine tools to China. According to the U.S. Census Bureau, more than 91,000 factories closed in the United States, between 1997 and 2018.

In 2013, a group of economists found that the China Shock reduced manufacturing employment in the United States by 55%. This was a loss of 982,000 manufacturing jobs. Wages for both manufacturing and non-manufacturing jobs fell in the United States.

A second study found that the United States lost an additional 2 million jobs between 1997 and 2011, due to increased imports from China. Employees working in textiles, footwear, and computer/electronic parts were particularly affected.

With each closed factory, the United States grew weaker. More and more, the United States lacked the ability to produce products essential to the nation's defense. In 2009, economists Gary Pisano and Willy Shih published an article in the Harvard Business Review, which listed certain technologies that our nation cannot produce in large quantities. The list is surprisingly long. It includes:

> Compact fluorescent lighting; LCDs for monitors, TVs and handheld devices like mobile phones; electrophoretic displays; lithium ion, lithium polymer and NiMH batteries; advanced rechargeable batteries for hybrid vehicles; crystalline and polycrystalline silicon solar cells; inverters and power semiconductors for solar panels; desktop, notebook and netbook PCs; low-end servers; hard-disk drives; consumer networking gear such as routers, access point, and home set-top boxes; advanced composite used in sporting goods and other consumer gear; advanced ceramics and integrated circuit packaging.

This list should concern anyone with a little bit of common sense. The ability to manufacture high tech devices brings good wages, and a high standard of living. If America choses to close its electronics factories, and replace them with golf courses and shopping malls, then it is only a matter of time before our standard of living will fall to that of Africa. We, after all, are modeling our economy on Africa.

According to Forbes magazine, the loss of our industrial base makes it impossible for the United States to engage in advanced manufacturing. For example, according to Forbes, the U.S. company, Amazon, sources virtually all of the components for its Kindle electronic reader from overseas:

- The flex circuit connectors come from China. This is because the U.S. supplier base for electronics moved to Asia.
- The electrophoretic display comes from Taiwan, which has expertise in this area.
- The injection-molded case is made in China. The United States lost the ability to mass produce plastics when our nation's toy, consumer electronics, and computer industries moved to Asia.
- The wireless card comes from South Korea, which specializes in the production of mobile phones.
- The controller board is made in China.
- The lithium ion battery is also from China, which has a large battery industry.

According to the Wall Street Journal, Apple Computers has difficulty assembling its Mac Pro computer in Texas because the company has difficulty obtaining a basic screw in the United States. In China, Apple can source vast quantities of custom-made screws on short notice. In the United States, Apple's supplier can only produce 1,000 screws per day.

According to economists Pisano and Shih, the United States has lost its technological edge, due to the loss of the industrial base. According to Pisano and Shih:

> The decline of manufacturing in a region sets off a chain reaction. Once manufacturing is outsourced,

process-engineering expertise can't be maintained, since it depends on daily interactions with manufacturing. Without process-engineering capabilities, companies find it increasingly difficult to conduct advanced research on next-generation process technologies. Without the ability to develop such new processes, they find they can no longer develop new products. In the long term, an economy that lacks an infrastructure for advanced process engineering and manufacturing will lose its ability to innovate.

In other words, when the United States lacks manufacturing, our nation lacks engineers, and insight as to how to improve products. This is why China produces electric cars that have left the United States in the dust.

An electric car made in the United States typically takes hours to charge, often the entire night. In comparison, China's leading electric vehicle manufacturer – BYD – can charge a car in about five to six minutes. This far exceeds current mainstream capabilities.

Strong dollar – weak United States.

The China shock was made possible because China and the United States were pursuing different strategies regarding the value of their currencies. China kept its currency artificially low, by means of a peg to the U.S. dollar. The United States, on the other hand, kept its currency artificially high, due to the petrodollar.

Between 2001 and 2009, President George W. Bush frequently expressed support for a strong dollar. According to Bush, a strong dollar was "in our nation's interests." Bush, of course, was selling a load of malarky to the American people. He was well-aware that America's industrial base was rapidly shrinking. Our nation's electricity consumption dropped, for the first time in a century, in 2005, due to the nation's de-industrialization.

As the Fortune 500 moved jobs offshore, our nation has grown progressively poorer. As of 2023, 42.1 million Americans are receiving food stamps. That is about 12.6% of the population. This is more than double the number in 2001, when George W. Bush took office. According to the Wall Street Journal, nearly half of our nation's population receives some sort of government assistance. The Journal notes that this is a historic high.

However, for many years, few people in the United States were willing to challenge the prevailing narrative. The media, U.S. politicians, and businesses all preached the benefits of a "strong dollar" and "free trade." Meanwhile, America's workers were left to fend for themselves, in communities bereft of factories. Our nation's politicians suggested "job training," when the only jobs in many communities were at Walmart.

Since the year 2000, the United States has been able to survive – without a dramatic drop in our standard of living – because of the petrodollar monopoly.

Rather than making goods, the United States "makes" dollars, and exports them to the world for whatever our nation needs. Petrodollars flow out, and imported cars, computers, cell phones, clothing, and food flow into the United States.

Since 1980, America's politicians have taken advantage of the strong dollar, and printed money with abandon. They were able to do so, because the dollar remained rock solid, due to the oil monopoly.

Below is a chart of the United States federal budget deficit from 1986 to the present.

Table 5.6

United States Federal Budget Deficit

Fiscal Year	Deficit ($ billions)	Debt to GDP Ratio
1986	$221	4.8%
1987	$150	3.1%
1988	$155	3.0%
1989	$153	2.7%
1990	$221	3.7%
1991	$269	4.4%
1992	$290	4.5%
1993	$255	3.7%
1994	$203	2.8%
1995	$164	2.1%
1996	$107	1.3%
1997	$ 22	0.3%
1998	($ 69)	(0.8%)
1999	($126)	(1.3%)
2000	($236)	(2.3%)
2001	($128)	(1.2%)
2002	$158	1.4%
2003	$378	3.3%
2004	$413	3.4%
2005	$318	2.4%
2006	$248	1.8%

2007	$161	1.1%
2008	$459	3.1%
2009	$1,413	9.8%
2010	$1,294	8.6%
2011	$1,300	8.3%
2012	$1,077	6.6%
2013	$680	4.0%
2014	$485	2.8%
2015	$442	2.4%
2016	$585	3.1%
2017	$665	3.4%
2018	$779	3.8%
2019	$984	4.6%
2020	$3,132	15.0%
2021	$2,772	12.1%
2022	$1,400	5.5%
2023	$1,700	6.3%
2024	$1,800	6.4%

Between 1986 and 2024, the federal government has borrowed progressively larger amounts, in terms of the size of the economy.

Clinton briefly balanced the budget in the late 1990s, due to pressure from Ross Perot. However, those gains were not to last. Following the events of 911, in September 2001, President George W. Bush used deficit spending to fund his wars in Iraq and Afghanistan. These wars pushed the federal budget back into the red, to the tune of 3% of GDP.

Serious problems began to emerge with the financial crisis of 2008. In that year, the housing market collapsed, creating widespread problems in the banking and mortgage sectors. The federal government printed billions of dollars to keep the U.S. economy afloat. Between 2009 and 2011, the Obama administration ran a federal deficit of between 8% and 10% of the nation's GDP. The system did not break, because those printed dollars remained convertible to oil.

During the covid crisis of 2020 to 2022, the government borrowed between 12% and 15% of the nation's GDP. Each time, the dollar was bolstered by the petrodollar arrangement with the Middle East oil producers.

Economist Robert Triffin predicted that the world would eventually reject the dollar, in the same way that the planet rejected the British pound in 1971. When this happens, it is foreseeable that the U.S. dollar will fall in value. Let's take a closer look at monopolies, to see how the loss of the petrodollar could affect the United States.

CHAPTER 6
The New Confederacy

In eastern Turkey, there is an abandoned city called Ani. Ani was the capital of ancient Armenia. Little remains of the city today, other than a few ancient churches and piles of bricks.

In its heyday, about 1,000 years ago, Ani was an important city on the Silk Road. It was known as the "City of 1,001 Churches." More than 100,000 people lived there. Each day, hundreds of camels would pass through Ani's gates, carrying silk, porcelain and spices from the east, in exchange for gold and products from the west.

Armenia's control of the Silk Road brought power and wealth. Ani was able to tax caravans passing through the region. This brought Armenia into conflict with its neighbors.

In 1064, a Persian army attacked Ani, intent on eliminating the Armenians' tolls on the route to the sea. The Persians captured the city. According to the Turkish historian Sibt ibn al-Jawzi, the Persians took at least 50,000 prisoners, after killing a similar number in the battle.

Between 1124 and 1209, Ani changed hands at least five more times, as the regional powers competed for control of the lucrative trade route. In 1226, a Mongol army swept out of China, and besieged the city. The Mongols attacked Ani for ten years, before finally conquering the city in 1236.

Despite all of these wars, Ani continued to thrive. It was always sustained by the wealth traveling on the Silk Road.

After the year 1500, conditions changed – Ani began to decline. By 1735, the city was completely abandoned.

In the first half of the 19th century, European travelers re-discovered the ruins of Ani. In academic journals and travel books, they described large public buildings and a well-preserved city wall. In the second half of the 19th century, an Armenian photographer published the first photos of the ruins.

Ani was a victim of changing trade routes. Ultimately, it wasn't the endless battles over eastern Turkey that destroyed Ani. It was technological change, that occurred 3,000 miles away, in western Europe. Portuguese explorer, Bartolomeu Dias, played a role in the destruction of Ani.

Bartolomeu Dias was born in 1450, in Portugal. He came from a noble family, that had a history of maritime expertise. By his mid-30s, Dias held a position on the royal court, where he supervised the royal warehouses.

King John II, of Portugal, asked Dias to find a sea route to India. The king wanted to avoid the expensive land routes through the Middle East, which were controlled by hostile powers. The Portuguese navy began to explore routes along the west coast of Africa, hoping to find a clear route to India.

In 1481, Dias participated in an expedition to the Gulf of Guinea, to construct a fort. This was approximately 2,000 miles south of Portugal, and about half-way down the coast of Africa.

As Portugal worked its way down the west coast of Africa, its explorers left stone markers, known as padräos, to mark their way. Padräos were stone pillars, often topped by a cross and the Portuguese coat of arms. They served as physical markers of areas explored, and claimed by Portugal.

In 1488, Dias became the first European to sail around the southern tip of Africa, known as the Cape of Good Hope. It took Portugal another nine years, before one of its ships finally made it to India. This was done in 1497, by Portuguese explorer Vasco da Gama.

This achievement broke Ani's monopoly on trade through eastern Turkey. It was now possible to sail a ship from Western Europe directly to India, without having to pay dozens of tolls to local rulers along the way. The price of Chinese and Indian goods in Europe fell dramatically.

Between 1500 and 1735, people left Ani, due to the lack of trade. Eventually, this once-powerful city became a pile of abandoned rocks, on a windswept plain.

The history of Ani shows what happens when a nation loses a monopoly on trade. Wealth no longer flows to that nation, making the region poorer.

In their book, Why Nation's Fail, Daron Acemoglu and James A. Robinson say that a nation faces a greater risk of failing if it relies upon an economy which is "extractive" in nature. An extractive economy is one that takes resources from other groups, by means of force or law.

This is often done by means of a monopoly.

A monopoly is a market structure where a single seller or producer controls the entire supply of a particular good or service, and there are no close substitutes available. For example, Ani had a monopoly on certain of the trade routes to China. There were no alternative suppliers, until Portugal broke the monopoly by means of the alternative sea route to India.

In their book, Acemoglu and Robinson explain how monopolies negatively affect a nation's economy. For example, suppose Mexico grants a legal monopoly to a friend of the president. The monopoly can be anything – cell phone service, a bus from the airport to city central, or a monopoly on a trash route. For each monopoly created, the Mexican economy gets weaker. The owner of the monopoly uses his legal control over the economy to extract resources from the population. While he gets richer, the people of Mexico become poorer.

Monopolies are a problem for several reasons. First, a monopoly can be a threat to a new technology. For example, the first power looms were delayed, because those who controlled the production of cloth in England and France didn't want to change the system. Acemoglu and Robinson argue that the industrial revolution occurred in England after 1688, because England abolished monopolies that year. As a result, entrepreneurs rushed into the field, and mechanized the process of making cloth.

Second, when a monopoly comes to an end, the cash flow formerly generated by the trade restriction also comes to an end. This can pose a threat to the persons who rely upon the monopoly.

Extractive institutions – such as monopolies – are artificial creations. They are not stable. They do not last long-term because they have to be held in place by force. Monopolies confiscate resources from weaker persons – or weaker societies – by means of guns, state power, or military power.

For example, for many years, England and France confiscated resources from weaker countries, by means of colonialism. Between 1800 and 1945, England colonized about 25% of the globe. A century ago, the British empire controlled half of Africa, half of the Middle East, all of India, and parts of China. France controlled much of West Africa, half of the Middle East, and much of southeast Asia.

Britain and France created these empires by means of military power, which was a result of the Industrial Revolution. This military power gave Britain and France the ability to exclude foreign trade from their empires. In other words, the British and the French empires were large-scale monopolies.

As we saw with Ani's monopoly on the Silk Road trade routes, monopolies have to be defended by military force. Other nations wanted access to the territories controlled by Britain and France. This included Germany, which only had a small number of colonies.

The conflict over colonies and foreign trade led to the two world wars, in the first half of the 20th century. As with the wars over the Silk Road, these wars were extremely bloody. Six percent of Britain's adult male population died in the First World War. France lost 17% of its male population, of fighting age. Germany lost over 2 million soldiers during the First World War alone. This was 15% of Germany's male population of fighting age.

At the end of the Second World War, 46% of the German male population, of military-age, was either killed or wounded.

At the end of the day, Britain and France lost their monopolies on trade. Both countries were economically exhausted by the conflict. This allowed the United States to assume world leadership in 1945. By 1960, the British and French empires were largely history.

When the British empire collapsed, the United Kingdom became poorer. Britain no longer had the ability to extract resources from its colonies, by means of a monopoly on trade.

This loss of cash flow had an effect on the British economy. The nation no longer had easy access to oil from the Middle East, coffee from East Africa, or tea from India. Instead of buying these goods for British pounds – which Britain could print – Britain had to trade to obtain these goods. The British pound predictably fell.

The British precedent poses lessons for the United States. Like Britain, the United States derives benefits from its monopoly on world trade, being conducted in U.S. dollars. Let's take a closer look at how the United States defends that monopoly.

CHAPTER 7
Defending the Dollar

As we have seen, extractive institutions must be maintained by force. This is true whether the extraction is being done by the Armenians in eastern Turkey, the British and French empires, or government monopolies in Mexico.

This book argues that America's near-monopoly on the sale of oil is an extractive institution. The extraction of value occurs as follows. About 80% of the world's oil trade is conducted exclusively with U.S. dollars. Suppose Vietnam needs oil for its economy. To purchase that oil, Vietnam must first trade goods to the United States, to acquire U.S. dollars. The United States prints those dollars at no cost to our nation, and then acquires say, $1 billion of Vietnamese rice. The rice comes to America, at no cost to the United States. Vietnam takes the dollars, and buys $1 billion of oil from Saudi Arabia, or another oil producing nation.

Now repeat this transaction dozens of times each day, for oil and other commodities traded on the planet. Each time, goods flow to the United States, with little value being delivered in return, except for printed U.S. dollars. This is how the United States is able to sustain a large and growing trade deficit.

It wasn't always this way. The United States used to have to work for a living.

Between 1870 and 1970, the United States had a positive balance of trade with the rest of the world. Our trade surplus averaged about 1.1% of U.S. GDP during the century leading up to 1970. We have seen how the United States became wealthy selling cars, oil, radios, and manufactured goods to the rest of the planet.

Things began to change in the mid-1970s. After Nixon established the petrodollar in 1974, the U.S. balance of trade began to deteriorate. Below is a chart of the trade balance, as a percentage of GDP, from 1970 to 2024:

Table 7.1

U.S. Balance of Trade

Year	Billions of US $	% of GDP
1970	$3.95	0.37%
1971	$0.62	0.05%
1972	$-3.37	-0.26%
1973	$4.11	0.29%
1974	$-0.82	-0.05%
1975	$15.98	0.95%
1976	$-1.63	-0.09%
1977	$-23.09	-1.11%
1978	$-25.37	-1.08%
1979	$-22.55	-0.86%
1980	$-13.06	-0.46%
1981	$-12.52	-0.39%
1982	$-19.97	-0.60%
1983	$-51.64	-1.42%

Year	Amount	Percent
1984	$-102.73	-2.54%
1985	$-114.02	-2.63%
1986	$-131.87	-2.88%
1987	$-144.77	-2.98%
1988	$-109.39	-2.09%
1989	$-86.74	-1.54%
1990	$-77.85	-1.31%
1991	$-28.61	-0.46%
1992	$-34.74	-0.53%
1993	$-65.17	-0.95%
1994	$-92.49	-1.27%
1995	$-89.76	-1.17%
1996	$-96.38	-1.19%
1997	$-101.97	-1.19%
1998	$-162.71	-1.80%
1999	$-259.55	-2.69%
2000	$-381.07	-3.72%
2001	$-376.75	-3.56%
2002	$-439.75	-4.02%
2003	$-521.96	-4.56%
2004	$-634.14	-5.19%
2005	$-739.90	-5.67%
2006	$-786.45	-5.69%
2007	$-735.93	-5.08%
2008	$-740.87	-5.02%
2009	$-419.15	-2.90%
2010	$-532.31	-3.54%

2011	$-579.62	-3.72%
2012	$-551.62	-3.39%
2013	$-479.39	-2.85%
2014	$-510.04	-2.91%
2015	$-526.20	-2.89%
2016	$-506.25	-2.71%
2017	$-539.93	-2.77%
2018	$-596.19	-2.90%
2019	$-596.26	-2.79%
2020	$-651.19	-3.12%
2021	$-845.05	-3.70%
2022	$-945.30	-3.70%
2023	$-773.40	-2.80%
2024	$-918.40	-3.10%
CUMULATIVE TRADE DEFICIT		$9.3 trillion

The above chart shows how the petrodollar has enabled the United States to run unrestricted trade deficits for fifty years. In 1977, the United States trade deficit was $23 billion, equal to about 1% of the size of the economy. Ten years later, in 1987, the trade deficit reached $144 billion, equal to 3% of our nation's GDP. By 2007, the deficit was $736 billion, and had reached 5% of GDP.

As John Maynard Keynes predicted in 1944, the United States is consuming the world's goods for free, in exchange for printed dollars. Monopolies are great, if you have the military power to enforce them.

Predictably, the United States defends this monopoly by means of military force. After U.S. Secretary of State Heny Kissinger struck his deal with the Saudis, the United States moved aggressively into the Middle East to defend the oil monopoly. Today, the United States maintains 40,000 to 50,000 troops in the Middle East. These troops are stationed at a wide array of military bases, located in the oil producing regions of the area.

In Bahrain, the United States took over Britain's naval base, formerly known as "HMS Jaffair." The base – now known as Naval Support Activity, Bahrain (NSA Bahrain) – is the headquarters of the Navy's 5th Fleet. According to a U.S. government website, NSA Bahrain "covers the busiest 152 acres in the world," providing support to ships and remote sites throughout the region. The 5th Fleet has about 28,000 employees in Bahrain, Kuwait and Qatar.

In Qatar, the United States established operations at the Al Udeid Air Base. The base is home to contingents from the U.S. Air Force and Britain's Royal Air Force, as well as the Qatari Air Force. As of June 2017, about 11,000 American military personnel worked at the base – a sizable number. In June 2025, Iran targeted the Al Udeid Air Base, as part of its war with Israel.

In 1977, the United States established a major naval base on an island in the Indian ocean. The base – known as Naval Support Facility, Diego Garcia – provides support for U.S. forces in the Indian Ocean and Persian Gulf. The base has port facilities, an airfield used by the U.S. Air Force and Navy, and a sophisticated radar, space tracking, and communications center. The base is capable of bombing sites in Afghanistan, Iran and the Middle East.

In Kuwait – on the northern end of the Persian Gulf – the United States maintains at least five military installations. These include Camp Arifjan, which is a forward headquarters of U.S. Army Central Command. The United States also maintains forces at the Ali Al Salem Air Base, near the Iraq border. The base, known as "The Rock," is known for its remote and rugged terrain. The United States also maintains Camp Buehring, in Kuwait. This base serves as a staging area for army units deploying to Iraq and Syria.

In the United Arab Emirates, the United States operates the Ain Al Asad Air Base in western Anbar province. In 2020, Iran attacked the base with missiles, in retaliation for the U.S. killing of Iranian General Qasem Soleimani.

The United Arab Emirates (UAE) hosts American forces at the Al-Dhafra airbase. The United States uses the base for reconnaissance and intelligence gathering. The United States maintains advanced aircraft at the base, including F-22 Raptor stealth fighters and various surveillance planes, drones and AWACS.

In Saudi Arabia, the Prince Sultan Air Base serves as a forward headquarters for the U.S. Army Central Command. The United States also maintains personnel at Erskan Village, located near Riyadh.

In the Kurdistan region of Iraq, the United States stations about 2,500 troops at the Erbil Air Base. According to a congressional report, the base provides training, military intelligence, and logistical support in northern Iraq.

It's been said that the petrodollar and U.S. military supremacy are the opposite sides of the same coin. U.S. military supremacy in the Middle East enforces the petrodollar monopoly, by ensuring that oil trades only in U.S. dollars. Meanwhile, the petrodollar pays for U.S. military forces in the region.

Iraq threatens the dollar.

On August 2, 1990, Iraq invaded the oil-rich kingdom of Kuwait.

In response, the UN Security Council imposed sanctions on Iraq. The sanctions discouraged countries from purchasing Iraqi oil.

Iraq's invasion led to a brief "100-hour" war in which the United States led a coalition of forces to liberate Kuwait. Iraq withdrew from Kuwait on February 28, 1991, ending the war.

After the war, the UN sanctions on Iraq remained in place. The sanctions led to widespread hardship in Iraq, due to the lack of foreign exchange entering the country.

In 1995, the United Nations adopted an "Oil for Food Program," for Iraq. In theory, the program authorized Iraq to sell oil, in exchange for food and other items deemed to be of a non-threatening nature. Iraq sold oil under this program only for U.S. dollars. The dollars were then used to purchase food for the Iraqi people.

In October 2000, Iraq's leader, Saddam Hussein, asked the United Nations for authority to sell oil for euro, rather than U.S. dollars. Saddam told the UN that Iraq would sell no oil at all, if the UN did not approve his request. Saddam's request posed a quandary for the West. An Iraqi embargo of oil would have reduced world oil production by about 4.5%. This would have increased world oil prices. On November 1, 2000, the UN approved Saddam's request to sell Iraqi oil for euro.

Washington, D.C. was not pleased with Saddam's demand. U.S. leaders already saw Iraq as a threat. Now, Iraq's leader, Saddam, threated the petrodollar monopoly.

Saddam's switch to euro made a small dent in America's cash flow from the petrodollar. In 2000, Iraq produced about 2.5 million barrels of oil per day. At $20 to $30 per barrel, Saddam's switch to the euro reduced demand for the U.S. dollar by about $23 billion per year.

$23 billion was not peanuts. The United States wanted that money. In addition, Saddam's demand threatened the other the 95% of the world's oil market.

If the other 95% of the world market were to shift to pricing in euro, the United States would lose approximately $500 billion of demand for the dollar every year. This largess would flow to Western Europe, rather than to the United States. In the view of the American leaders, Saddam needed to be stopped.

After the attack on the World Trade Center, in September 2001, the United States promoted the idea that Iraq was involved in the attack. The claim was not true. However, the United States wanted a reason to remove Saddam from power.

President George W. Bush told the media that Saddam was building "weapons of mass destruction," which could not be tolerated. He said that the United States needed to remove Saddam from power.

On February 5, 2003, Bush sent his Secretary of State, Colin Powell, to the United Nations, to convince the body to approve an invasion. Powell spent an hour showing slides of Iraq's alleged weapons violations.

Most of the planet was unmoved by Powell's speech. Three of the five permanent members of the security council – China, Russia and France – opposed any resolution to authorize a war. In addition, many other countries – including Germany, Canada, Mexico and Indonesia – opposed an American invasion of Iraq.

France led a campaign against Bush's proposed invasion. France lobbied the UN Security Council to vote against any resolution authorizing the move. In doing so, the French leaders likely understood that Europe would have benefitted if Iraqi oil continued to trade for euro, rather than U.S. dollars.

France successfully blocked UN approval of the invasion. However, Bush went ahead with the war anyway, claiming that he only needed authorization from the U.S. Congress.

On March 19, 2003, the United States bombed key sites in Baghdad. The following day, the United States invaded Iraq. The invasion force consisted of 248,000 soldiers from the United States, and 47,000 British and Australian soldiers. 70,000 troops from Iraq's Kurdistan region supported the Anglo-American army.

The war was brief. On April 9, 2003, U.S. forces entered Baghdad, and ended Saddam's 24-year rule. American forces captured Saddam, and executed him in 2006.

After the invasion, Iraq quietly stopped selling oil for euro, and continued selling oil only for U.S. dollars. Thus, the petrodollar remained in place, as to Iraq.

Meanwhile, the United States seized control of Iraq's oil revenues.

On May 22, 2003, President Bush signed Executive Order 13303. The order placed Iraq's oil revenues under control of the United States. The order, entitled "Protection of the Development Fund for Iraq and Other Property in Which Iraq Has an Interest," required all of Iraq's oil revenue to be placed in an account at the Federal Reserve Bank in New York. Since 2003, every American president has renewed the executive order.

Since 2003, the United States has required Iraq's Ministry of Finance to submit requests for funds to the U.S. Treasury. The United States then decides whether to approve or deny the requests. If a request is approved, the United States allegedly flies pallets of cash to Baghdad. Iraq uses these payments to provide for the basic needs of its 40 million residents.

In 2010, the UN Security Council passed a resolution – Number 1956 – demanding the closure of the Development Fund for Iraq. The resolution called for the transfer of the fund to the Iraqi government by 2011. The United States has refused to comply with the resolution.

Since the invasion, it is estimated that the Federal Reserve Bank has collected $120 billion of Iraqi oil money. It is doubtful that all of this money has been released to Iraq.

Libya threatens the dollar.

The next attack on the petrodollar came from Libya. Libya is the 7th largest oil producer in OPEC. It produces about 1.5% of world oil production each year.

Libya's leader – Muammar Gaddafi – took a keen interest in currency. In 2009, Gaddafi proposed to sell oil for a new currency to be called the "gold dinar". The gold dinar would be backed by gold, oil and other commodities from Africa. It is unclear whether Gaddafi intended to issue the currency from Libya, or a pan-African entity. The idea was to free Africa from selling commodities in U.S. dollars and French francs, at the expense of the African people.

Gaddafi's proposal was met with resistance from Europe and the United States. The Western powers did not like Libya selling its resources for a currency that they did not control.

In late 2010, a series of pro-democracy protests broke out in North Africa. This became known as the "Arab Spring" movement. The leaders of the movement sought to challenge authoritarian governments in the Arab world.

In 2011, the Arab Spring movement challenged Gaddafi's government. The protests soon evolved into a civil war against Gaddafi. The United States and France provided military support for the popular forces fighting Gaddafi.

On March 17, 2011, the UN security council called for a "no fly" zone over Libya. Ostensibly, the resolution sought to protect civilians in the ongoing civil war. In reality, the Western powers used the resolution to shut down the Iraqi air force, which Gaddafi still controlled.

Two days later, on March 19, 2011, a NATO-led coalition began to enforce the "no fly" zone. The coalition consisted of forces from Britain, France, the United States, Belgium, Canada, Denmark, Spain and Italy.

Over eight months, NATO forces flew 26,500 missions in Libya. This included 7,000 bombing sorties targeting Gaddafi's forces.

In August 2011, Libya's capital, Tripoli, fell to forces controlled by the opposition National Transition Council. Gaddafi fled the capital, and sought to reestablish his government in the south of the country.

On October 20, 2011, a NATO aircraft fired on a convoy carrying Gaddafi and his loyalist forces. During the exchange, forces opposed to Gaddafi's government killed Gaddafi. From the point of view of the West, the war was over. Gaddafi no longer posed a threat to the U.S. dollar or the euro in Africa. On October 31, the UN security council unanimously voted to end NATO's involvement in the war.

The international community left Libya in ruins. The country now has two competing governments. The international community recognizes the Government of National Unity, which controls the western part of the country. Eastern Libya is governed by the Government of National Stability. Both governments rely upon militias, which control different parts of the country.

Since Gaddafi's death in 2011, there has been no further discussion of selling Libyan oil for an alternative African currency.

Venezuela threatens the dollar.

Venezuela has the world's largest proven reserves of oil. It is estimated that Venezuela has 304 billion barrels of oil – about 18% of the world's known reserves.

On September 8, 2017, Venezuela's president, Nicolas Maduro, announced that Venezuela would sell oil for currencies other than the U.S. dollar. During his press conference, Maduro said that he would sell oil for Chinese yuan, the Japanese yen, the Russian ruble, and the Indian rupee.

The United States responded by sanctioning Venezuela.

On January 28, 2019, the United States targeted Venezuela's national oil company, Petróleos de Venezuela, S.A. (PDVSA). The United States froze $7 billion of the company's assets. The sanctions prevented American companies from paying PDVSA for oil that they had already received from Venezuela.

The United States also sanctioned more than 150 other companies and individuals in Venezuela's petroleum, mining, and banking industries.

Venezuelan oil production collapsed. Between 2016 and 2020, the nation's oil production fell from nearly 2.5 million barrels per day, to just over half a million barrels per day – an 80% reduction. Venezuela lost more than $11 billion in 2019 alone, due to the sanctions.

In August 2019, the United States froze Venezuelan government assets, in American jurisdiction. Britain and Portugal joined the sanctions. Altogether, the three countries seized more than $6 billion.

Venezuela began to experience shortages of milk, meat, coffee, rice, oil, flour, butter, toilet paper, and medicines.

The shortages led to one of the largest refugee crises in the Americas, with millions of Venezuelans fleeing the country. The United Nations estimated that more than five million people left the country as a result of the collapse – more than 15% of the nation's population.

By 2023, those remaining in Venezuela experienced a 73% drop in their standard of living. According to the UN, nearly 82% of the country now lives in poverty. Many compare the collapse to the aftermath of a major war.

America is vulnerable.

The examples of Iraq, Libya and Venezuela show that it would be foolhardy for any single country to try and supplant the U.S. oil monopoly.

As of 2025, the United States is too powerful, militarily and economically. The United States can easily destroy an entire country – through bombs or economic warfare – if that country challenges the petrodollar monopoly.

However, America's power has not stopped others from trying.

As explained below, the petrodollar is vulnerable, and could soon be part of history. China and Russia are assembling an alliance that will have the ability to destroy the petrodollar, in a turnkey fashion.

If this happens, the value of the dollar could collapse overnight. As we saw with the medieval city of Ani, the United States could be plunged into poverty.

CHAPTER 8

Countermeasures
– BRICS

The Russians were the first to identify the weakness of the dollar.

In 1998, a Russian political science professor – Igor Nikolaevich Panarin – predicted that the United States would disintegrate prior to 2010. Panarin based his conclusions on classified information about the United States economy, obtained by the Russian intelligence community.

In an interview with the Russian publication Izvestia, Panarin stated that "the U.S. dollar isn't secured by anything. The country's foreign debt has grown like an avalanche; this is a pyramid, which has to collapse."

Panarin initially received little attention for his claim. However, Russian state media began to publicize his claim in 2009, after every bank on Wall Street nearly went bankrupt during the 2008 financial crisis.

In March 2009, Panarin gave a speech at the Diplomatic Academy of the Ministry of Foreign Affairs, in Moscow. During that speech, Panarin repeated his prediction that the United States would collapse. He said that Russia and China would soon be world powers. As such,

Russia and China would need to collaborate to rebuild the world economy with a new currency once the U.S. dollar declined, and the United States either ceased to exist or was seriously impaired. According to Panarin, Alaska could return to Russian control following any such collapse.

On March 16, 2009, Russia called for a new international reserve currency at the G20 summit.

A week later, China joined Russia in calling for reform. On March 23, 2009, the President of the People's Bank of China, Zhou Xiaochuan, called for a new world's currency, to replace the dollar. Zhou argued that a new reserve currency would "significantly reduce the risks of a future crisis." Zhou suggested that the IMF's special drawing rights (a currency basket then comprising dollars, euros, sterling and yen) could serve as a super-sovereign reserve currency, saying that it would not be easily influenced by the policies of individual countries.

On March 26, 2009, a panel of experts considered the threats posed by the dollar as a reserve currency. During the conference, one of the panel members, Joseph Stiglitz, said:

> The system in which the dollar is the reserve currency is a system that has long been recognized to be unsustainable in the long run. It's a system that is fraying, but as it frays it can contribute a great deal to global instability.

The Stiglitz panel called for a new international reserve asset to mitigate the instability caused by the growing overhang of United States dollars, in the world economy.

Russian President Vladimir Putin joined the calls for reform. In a speech to a pro-Kremlin youth group, Putin called the United States a "parasite" on the world economy. According to Putin, "They are living beyond their means and shifting a part of the weight of their problems to the world economy. They are living like parasites off the global economy and their monopoly of the dollar."

Russia and China sought support for their views from the international community. On June 16, 2009, the leaders of Brazil, Russia, India and China met for a formal summit in Yekaterinburg, Russia. These nations were already known on Wall Street by the acronym "BRIC", from the first letter of each of the four nations.

At the summit, the BRIC leaders discussed setting up a new financial architecture for the world.

Following the summit, the BRIC nations called for a new global reserve currency, to reduce to risk of a collapsing dollar. According to the BRIC members, the new global currency should be "diverse, stable and predictable." In making this recommendation, it is likely that the BRIC members were influenced by the recommendations of John Maynard Keynes, at the Bretton Woods conference, and the later writings of economist, Robert Triffin.

In 2011, South Africa joined the BRIC alliance, changing the group's acronym to "BRICS".

In 2014, BRICS set up a new bank, called the New Development Bank, to provide loans for the BRICS members. The bank's headquarters is located in Shanghai, China.

BRICS also took steps to facilitate international monetary transfers, through a platform that is not reliant on the U.S. dollar. The bloc has put significant resources into two different platforms. Russia is developing a system called "BRICS Pay". China, Thailand and the United Arab Emirates are developing a system called "BRICS Bridge", formerly known as M-Bridge. Both systems compete with the SWIFT system, operated by the West.

Russia sells its treasury bonds.

In 2014, the United States and Russia fell into conflict over the Crimean peninsula, located on the north coast of the Black Sea.

The peninsula has long been of key importance to Russian national security. Russia annexed the Crimean peninsula in 1783. The following year, Russia built a naval base at Sevastopol, on the peninsula. The base is the home of the Russian Black Sea Fleet.

Following the disintegration of the Soviet Union in 1991, the Russian naval base fell into the hands of Ukraine. Ukraine, however, was not a stable country. The country is made up of two different ethnic groups, at war with each other. The eastern portion of the country is Russian, and speaks Russian.

The western portion of Ukraine speaks Ukrainian, a different language. The Ukrainian portion of the country is bitterly opposed to Russian control of the country. This animosity goes back, at least, to the 1930s, when Russia engineered a famine in the eastern part of Ukraine, as part of its colonization of the country.

In 2013, Ukrainian President Viktor Yanukovych indicated that he supported closer ties between his country and Russia. Yanukovych indicated that he did not want Ukraine to join the European Union. Yanukovych's decision led to protests in Kiev. In February 2014, Yanukovych was forced to flee the country, after the protests turned violent.

On February 27, 2014, Russia seized control of the Crimean parliament, and key government buildings. Soon, Russia controlled the entire Crimean peninsula.

In March 2014, the United States imposed sanctions on top Russian officials, in retaliation for Russia's seizure of Crimea. The United States also sought to isolate Russia financially. The Obama administration blocked Russia from participating in the G-8 financial summit. Obama also froze the financial accounts of several prominent Russians, and restricted their travel. As a result, the ruble fell against the dollar, and the Russian stock market plummeted.

Russia threatened to retaliate with financial means. Putin's adviser, Serge Glazyev, told the press:

> We hold a decent amount of Treasury bonds – more than $200 billion – and if the United States dares to

freeze accounts of Russian businesses and citizens, we can no longer view America as a reliable partner. We will encourage everybody to dump U.S. Treasury bonds, get rid of dollars as an unreliable currency, and leave the U.S. market.

When Glazyev made these comments, Russia was selling oil and natural gas to the West, for U.S. dollars. Russia had previously invested its earnings in U.S. treasury bonds. In 2014, Russia began to dump the bonds. Below is a chart showing the decline in Russia's ownership of U.S. treasury bonds:

Table 8.1

Russian holdings of U.S. Treasury Bonds

Month & Year	Holdings ($ billions)
Jan. 2007	8.5
Dec. 2007	32.7
Jan. 2008	35.2
Dec. 2008	116.4
Jan. 2009	119.6
Dec. 2009	141.8
Jan. 2010	124.2
Dec. 2010	151
Jan. 2011	139.3
Dec. 2011	149.5
Jan. 2012	145.7
Dec. 2012	161.5
Jan. 2013	164.4
Feb. 2013	164.9

Dec. 2013	138.6
Jan. 2014	131.8
Dec. 2014	86.0
Jan. 2015	82.2
Dec. 2015	92.1
Jan. 2016	96.9
Dec. 2016	86.1
Jan. 2017	86.2
Dec. 2017	102.5
Jan. 2018	96.9
Mar. 2018	96.1
April 2018	48.7
May 2018	14.9
Dec. 2018	13.2

The chart shows how the Obama administration squandered Russian goodwill, towards the United States. In 2012, Russia held over $160 billion of treasury bonds. Six years later, Russia had virtually none.

The United States did not take Russia's warning seriously. The word on Wall Street was that Russia was too small to affect the market for treasury bonds, or the value of the dollar. However, some analysts worried how China would react. According to Eugene Chausovsky, a senior Eurasia analyst at consulting firm Stratfor, "If we had this kind of sell-off from China, this would be a completely different picture."

The rise of BRICS.

Between 2017 and 2021, President Trump kept the situation in Ukraine under control. Trump respected Russian interests in the region. He took no steps to bring Ukraine into either NATO or the European Union. In return, Russia took no steps to encourage a growing civil war in the eastern provinces of Ukraine.

That all changed with the inauguration of President Joe Biden, in January 2021. Biden believed that Ukraine should be part of the European Union (EU), and if possible, a member of NATO.

Russia repeatedly warned the United States it would not accept Ukraine becoming a member of NATO. Ukraine was too close to Moscow – about 460 miles. Russia would never accept Western weapons this close to its capital.

The United States and Russia had previously had this conversation, sixty years earlier, in October 1962. In that month, U.S. President John Kennedy told Russia that he would not accept Russian weapons in Cuba, 90 miles off the American coast. Russian President Nikita Khruschev told Kennedy that he was not happy with American "Jupiter" missiles in Turkey, on Russia's border. Both the Russian missiles and the American missiles could be armed with nuclear weapons.

In October 1962, Kennedy and Khruschev agreed not to place offensive weapons on each other's border. Khruschev agreed to remove Russia's missiles from Cuba. In return, Kennedy agreed to remove the U.S. Jupiter missiles from Turkey.

Everyone was happy until President Biden violated the agreement. Biden insisted on having Ukraine join NATO. Doing so, raised the possibility of the West placing offensive weapons on Russia's border, in Ukraine.

In 2022, the conflict between Russia and the United States over Ukraine came to blows. On February 24, Russia invaded Ukraine, with the intent to quickly seize Kiev, and take control of the country.

The United States and NATO responded with a raft of financial sanctions against Russia. On February 26, the United States, EU, Britain and Canada blocked most Russian banks from using the SWIFT financial transfer system. The SWIFT system uses electronic messages to implement international transfers of money and securities. By excluding Russia from SWIFT, the United States sought to prevent international buyers from paying for Russian oil.

Two days later, the same group of nations, together with Japan, froze approximately $280 billion of foreign reserves held by the Russian Central Bank. The United States and EU later used Russia's confiscated assets to provide collateral for a loan to Ukraine.

The West's confiscation of Russia's foreign reserves set off alarm bells in the world's financial circles. The event was unprecedented. The United States had previously frozen the assets of countries. However, these actions involved smaller nations, such as Vietnam, Iran and Venezuela. Never before had the United States targeted the assets of a large country, such as Russia.

On the internet, people began to chatter about possible ways of defeating U.S. financial hegemony. One of the proposed methods was to expand BRICS, issue a new reserve currency, and then have the expanded BRICS membership simultaneously reject the dollar. If this were to occur, then the value of the dollar would fall, potentially, by 50%.

If the dollar fell by 50%, then prices of imported goods in the United States would double. If the dollar fell by 80%, then prices of goods imported to the United States would increase five-fold, or by 500%.

The consequences could be catastrophic to the United States. The United States imports approximately 35% of the oil that it consumes. If the price of that oil were to double or triple, life in the United States could become very difficult. As we have seen, the United States also imports large amounts of food. If food prices were to double, the United States could experience riots, and possible food rationing.

In June 2022, Russian President Putin announced that BRICS intended to establish a new reserve currency. The value of the new currency would be based on a basket of currencies from its member nations. The following year, BRICS announced that in intended to invite other countries to join the alliance.

Thus, BRICS began to implement the two steps necessary to replace the U.S. dollar:

1. BRICS started work on a new reserve currency; and
2. The alliance began to expand membership.

In August 2023, BRICS announced that it had invited six new countries to join the group of nations. These were Argentina, Egypt, Ethiopia, Iran, Saudi Arabia, and the United Arab Emirates (UAE).

In January 2024, four of these countries joined the bloc. These were Egypt, Ethiopia, Iran, and the UAE. Argentina did not join, following a change in its government. Saudi Arabia indefinitely postponed a decision to join.

The expansion of BRICS in 2024 significantly strengthened the alliance. Iran and the UAE gave BRICS greater control over the world's oil production. Egypt gave the bloc access to the Red Sea shipping route between Europe and Asia.

The following year, BRICS grew stronger.

On October 24, 2024, BRICS invited thirteen additional countries to join, as "partner countries." These were Algeria, Belarus, Bolivia, Cuba, Indonesia, Kazakhstan, Malaysia, Nigeria, Thailand, Turkey, Uganda, Uzbekistan and Vietnam. These nations formally joined the bloc in January 2025. Indonesia joined the alliance as a full member, bringing the total number of full members to eleven.

As of mid-2025, the BRICS alliance boasts of some astonishing numbers. The alliance accounts for 25% of the earth's land mass and 54% of the world's population. The BRICS countries have a combined population of 4.3 billion. BRICS includes seven of the ten most populous countries on earth.

The BRICS economies constitute about 42% of world GDP. BRICS controls 41% of the planet's oil output and 45% of global agricultural production. This includes 42% of the world's wheat production, 52% of rice production, and 46% of soybean production.

The chart below shows the percentage of world oil production controlled by each BRIC member, as of mid-2025:

Table 8.2

BRICS' Percentage of World Oil Production

Name	OPEC Member	Oil Production (million bpd)	Share of World Oil Production
Brazil	No	3.62	4.4%
Russia	No	10.32	12.5%
India	No	--	--
China	No	4.16	5.0%
South Africa	No	--	--
Egypt	No	0.50	0.6%
Ethiopia	No	--	--
Iran	Yes	4.00	4.8%

UAE	Yes	3.22	3.9%
Algeria	Yes	1.41	1.7%
Belarus	No	--	--
Bolivia	No	--	--
Cuba	No	0.04	--
Indonesia	No	0.61	0.7%
Kazakhstan	No	1.88	2.3%
Malaysia	No	2.00	2.4%
Nigeria	Yes	1.80	2.1%
Thailand	No	--	--
Turkey	No	--	--
Uganda	No	--	--
Uzbekistan	No	--	--
Vietnam	No	0.40	0.5%
TOTALS		33.96	41.2%

If we add Saudi Arabia's oil production – of 10.3 million barrels per day – to the BRICS numbers, then the alliance will control 53.7% of global oil production.

Collectively, BRICS is growing faster than the West. Economists estimate that the nations comprising BRICS will grow by about 4.8% per year, for the foreseeable future. This is three times faster than the estimated growth of the G7 nations, which includes the United States. The G7 is growing at only about 1.5%.

Thus, BRICS is a game-changer, in terms of international power. For the first time since the end of World War II, a group of nations – acting as an alliance – has the ability to challenge U.S. hegemony on the planet.

By the stroke of a pen, the BRICS nations could collectively adopt a new currency, and price oil exclusively in the new currency. If BRICS were to do so, the U.S. dollar would be rendered obsolete, as a tool for doing business on much of the planet.

In other words, the United States has an Achilles heel. Russia and China are aware of the weakness, and are taking steps to exploit it. Americans need to know that our nation's grasp on world power is failing, and that our standard of living could be wiped out overnight.

CHAPTER 9
Defending the Kingdom With Tariffs

Our nation has a long history of using tariffs to protect American industry.

A tariff is a tax imposed by a government on goods imported from another country. Tariffs make imported goods more expensive. This protects local industries and jobs from foreign competition.

President George Washington was an early supporter of tariffs. In his 1790 State of the Union Address, Washington argued that tariffs were necessary to protect the nation. He said:

> A free people ought not only to be armed, but disciplined; . . . and their safety and interest require that they should promote such manufactures as tend to render them independent of others for essential, particularly military, supplies.

Alexander Hamilton, the first Secretary of the Treasury, strongly supported tariffs. In his Report on Manufactures, Hamilton called for custom barriers to protect infant industries. Hamilton argued that goods would ultimately become cheaper if they were made in the United States, even if they were initially more expensive due to the tariff.

The United States first imposed large protective tariffs on manufactured goods as a result of the War of 1812. The War of 1812 was a conflict between the United States and Britain, between the years 1812 and 1815. The United States fought the war because the British navy was forcing U.S. sailors to work on its ships. Britain also provided arms to American Indians.

During the war, our nation quickly learned that Britain was far more industrialized than the United States. Britain had steel mills, and could produce guns more quickly and cheaply than the United States. This made a difference in the war. During the war, Britain invaded Washington, D.C., and burned the White House.

After the war, Congress passed the Tariff of 1816, to protect U.S. industry. The Act imposed a 25% tax on all wool and cotton goods imported into the United States. Essentially, the tariff targeted manufactured textiles from England. At that time, England had mechanical looms powered by steam and water. The United States had none. The United States produced textiles by hand, a slow and laborious process.

As a result of the tariff, the United States quickly replicated the British power looms. Francis Cabot Lowell, a Boston merchant, memorized the design of the power loom, and brought the technology to the United States from England. Lowell did this by carefully observing the workings of the looms during a trip to England. Soon, the northeast United States was competing with Britain in the manufacture and sale of cloth.

During the years before the Civil War, the United States continued to debate the merits of tariffs. In 1841, a German economist – writing in the United States – published a highly-influential book in support of tariffs. The economist, Friedrich List, was a newspaper editor in Pennsylvania. His book, The National System of Political Economy, is, in my opinion, the most persuasive argument for tariffs ever written.

In the book, List described the history of trade policy, going back 500 years, to the 1300s. List described how the Venetians and Dutch protected their markets, and their shipping industries. He describes how Britain acquired industry, by attracting skilled merchants from Holland and Germany, in the 1500s. The book is astonishing to read, even today.

List's contemporary, Abraham Lincoln, also favored protective tariffs. Lincoln famously argued that when Americans bought U.S.-made goods, both the goods and the money remained within the United States, and benefitted the country. When Americans bought foreign-made goods, the money went overseas.

In the mid-19th century, American tariffs were among the lowest in the world, averaging about 17%. During his campaign for president in 1860, Lincoln supported higher tariffs in the United States.

In March 1861, Congress passed the Morrill Tariff. The tariff increased import duties by 70%. The tariff increased import taxes on British iron, clothing, and manufactured goods, provoking outrage in England. When the British House of Lords condemned the tariff, the American Congress was not amused. The Senate Finance Committee chairman responded, "What right has a foreign country to make any question about what we choose to do?"

Between 1861 and 1933, the United States had one of the highest average tariff rates on manufactured goods in the world. During this period, average tariffs in the United States were 50%. From 1871 to 1913, U.S. GDP grew about 4% annually. This was twice the growth rate of Britain, which preached free trade. America's growth was also well above the U.S. average in the 20th century.

By 1900, the United States had become highly industrialized. This industry, as we have seen, helped the United States win the First and Second World Wars. This was all the result of tariffs, which protected the United States economy from cheaper manufactured goods, made overseas.

The United States lowers its tariffs.

U.S. trade policy changed in 1913, following the electoral victory of the Democrats in 1912. In the following year, the United States reduced its average tariff on manufactured goods from 44% to 25%. At that point, the United States already had factories. We were trying to get other countries to reduce their tariffs, so that American businesses could increase sales overseas.

In 1934, Congress passed the Reciprocal Tariff Act of 1934. The Act authorized the president to negotiate reduced tariffs with other countries, provided that the reduction was mutual.

Between 1934 and 1945, the United States negotiated over 32 trade agreements with other countries, mutually reducing tariffs. These were known as "bilateral trade agreements."

Between 1948 and 1994, the United States promoted the reduction of tariffs through a forum known as the General Agreement on Tariffs and Trade (GATT). In each round of discussions, the United States negotiated progressively lower tariffs. We have seen how these negotiations led to NAFTA, and the export of American jobs to Mexico and China. By 2023, under the Biden Administration, tariffs in the United States were at a historic low.

Trump sounds the alarm.

In 2016, President Donald Trump began to call attention to the decline of the United States industrial base. Trump pointed out that our nation has virtually no ability to build a cell phone, flat screen television, or computer. He called for renegotiating NAFTA, or eliminating the treaty altogether. At a speech in Detroit, Michigan, Trump pointed to the urban decline that surrounded the viewing stand. He told the audience that Hillary Clinton and her husband, Bill Clinton, were responsible for such decline. "She did this to you," he said.

The American people responded by electing Trump in 2016, and again in 2024.

On April 2, 2025, Trump declared a national emergency, and announced a raft load of tariffs targeting the foreign goods coming into the United States. Since then, the Trump administration has been negotiating with the planet over the appropriate level of tariff to apply.

Trump keeps the petrodollar in place.

Both Trump and his Treasury Secretary, Scott Bessent, have repeatedly stated that they wish to keep the petrodollar in place.

Trump has been particularly concerned about BRICS' efforts to replace the U.S. dollar, with its own international currency. During the 2024 campaign, Trump threatened to impose a 100% tariff on any country that joined BRICS. In July 2025, Trump suggested a 10% tariff on countries joining the alliance.

Trump's decision to keep the petrodollar in place preserves American power. The United States will continue to have the ability to print a trillion dollars, and use the money to move chip factories from Taiwan, or to invade the Middle East.

However, the American people need to realize that Trump's decision comes with a cost.

As long as the petrodollar remains in place, the U.S. dollar will remain artificially overvalued. The petrodollar makes it difficult for American companies to manufacture profitably in the United States. In the past, America's automakers – Ford, GM and Stellantis – have survived by importing parts from Mexico and Canada. If Ford and GM are forced to make those parts in the United States, they may not be able to do so profitably.

In addition, as long as the dollar is artificially inflated by the oil monopoly, there is a risk that the value of the dollar could plummet in the future. As we have seen, this could occur if BRICS decides to price commodities, and oil, in a currency other than the dollar.

As explained below, a currency collapse could have catastrophic effects on the United States.

CHAPTER 10

Consequences

Beirut is located on the eastern end of Mediterranean sea. At the end of the First World War, the region fell under the control of France. During the 20th century, the region thrived. Photos of the city show a lush region, with high rise buildings surrounding the blue waters of the sea.

Beirut was once known as the "Paris of the Middle East." Due to its excellent weather, the region attracted tourists from Europe, particularly France. Beirut became a hub for tourism, finance, and intellectual life, with a thriving arts and entertainment scene.

From 1975 to 1990, Lebanon suffered a civil war. The war caused significant destruction, and large numbers of people left the country.

After the war, Lebanon relied on tourism, the sale of real estate, and remittances from the diaspora to survive. The country also sought to restore its banking sector, by offering high interest rates and secrecy to foreign depositors.

To provide stability to investors, Lebanon pegged its currency – the lira – to the U.S. dollar. For twenty years – from 1997 to 2019 – Lebanon maintained a fixed exchange rate -- 1,507.5 lira to the dollar.

However, beneath the surface, the country's finances were falling apart. Between 2007 and 2014, Lebanon's trade deficit tripled. The deficit was already at high levels, based on the nation's GDP. By 2014, Lebanon's trade deficit was equal to 32% of the country's GDP.

Meanwhile, Lebanon's government debt rapidly increased. Between 2012 and 2019, the nation's debt increased from 131% of GDP, to 172%.

Economists say that a country will experience financial problems when public debt is over 120% of GDP. That prediction held true in the case of Lebanon.

Between January 2023 and March 2024, Lebanon devalued its currency 98% against the dollar. In other words, the currency became essentially worthless. By early 2024, it took 90,000 lira to purchase one U.S. dollar. In other words, the cost of purchasing U.S. dollars increased by 59 times.

Needless to say, imported goods became prohibitively expensive, for persons earning Lebanese lira. Prices for local goods – denominated in lira – also increased.

Following the devaluation, the Lebanese government found it difficult to provide basic services. The government could not afford imported energy, to provide electricity. As a result, the government provided electricity only for one hour per day. Overnight, Beirut went dark. Those with access to foreign currency relied on generators for electricity.

Due to the lack of electricity, the government had difficulty providing water. Water requires electric pumps to purify and move the water. Lebanese were forced to drink water from the street, and other unsanitary places. This caused a cholera epidemic, for the first time in decades.

Lebanon previously relied on imported food for much of the nation's diet. Imported food is now prohibitively expensive. As a result, food is now scarce. Some parents left their children with orphanages, due to their inability to feed them.

Due to the lack of foreign currency, banks initially refused to return funds to their depositors. After the devaluation, some people resorted to armed robbery, to try and get their funds back from the banks.

What happened in Lebanon could happen in the United States. The markers are easy to read – high national debt and a dependence on imported goods.

The situation in Lebanon is not that different from that of our own country. In the United States, the federal debt is about 120% of the nation's GDP. That is where Lebanon's problems started. We, the American people, are on the cusp of a devaluation.

America, however, benefits from a significant difference. As of 2025, the United States still has a monopoly on the sale of oil – the petrodollar. However, if the petrodollar is lost to BRICS, the United States will have difficulty paying for imported goods. This is called a balance of payments crisis.

A balance of payments crisis occurs when a country's foreign exchange reserves are depleted, threatening its ability to finance essential imports, or to service its foreign debt. This usually results in a rapid devaluation of the country's currency.

In a balance of payments crisis, the United States will be defenseless. We have no foreign currency reserves to defend the U.S. dollar.

The risk of a currency collapse in the United States is real, and should not be underestimated. We have seen this story over and over again, in recent history.

Thailand – 1997

Between 1985 and 1996, Thailand's economy grew nearly 10% per year. On the surface, the country appeared to be an economic miracle. Thailand's growth rate was the highest in the world. Meanwhile, inflation remained low, at only 3% to 6% per year. The currency was also stable, pegged at 25 Thai baht to the dollar.

However, beneath the surface there were problems. In 1980, Thailand's external debt was only $8.3 billion. By 1995, Thailand owed foreigners $100 billion. Most of this borrowing was done by the private sector. In just three years – between 1993 and 1996 – Thailand's banks increased their external debt from 39% of GDP to 123% of GDP.

This debt fueled a surge of imports. In 1996, Thailand experienced a trade deficit equal to 9.1% of GDP.

These numbers were flashing a warning sign to the world's bankers.

On May 14, 1997, foreign hedge funds began to dump the Thai baht. The hedge funds thought that Thailand would have to devalue the currency, causing the value of the baht to drop.

On June 30, 1997, Thailand's prime minister, Chavalit Yongchaiyudh, said that he would not devalue the currency. However, Thailand lacked foreign reserves sufficient to support the currency peg.

On July 2, 1997, the Thai government was forced to float the baht. Over a few weeks, the baht lost more than half of its value.

Suddenly, the Thai people were plunged into poverty. The cost of imported goods in Thailand doubled overnight. The Thai stock market dropped 75%. The country's largest finance company, Finance One, collapsed.

Thailand's formerly-booming economy ground to a halt. The nation experienced massive layoffs in finance, real estate, and construction. Over 600,000 foreign workers left the country.

Thailand was the first domino to fall, in what became known as the Asian Financial Crisis. The crisis quickly spread to other countries in the region, including Indonesia, Malaysia, South Korea, and the Philippines. Each of these countries was forced to devalue its currency, leading to sharp declines in asset prices, and widespread recession.

CONSEQUENCES

Russia -- 1998

The Asian Financial Crisis created a ripple effect, that affected Russia the following year.

In the 1990s, Russia's economy was particularly weak. The country had only started recovering from 75 years of socialist rule, which had allowed much of the country's means of production to deteriorate.

To make matters worse, between December 1994 and August 1996, Russia fought a war with separatists in Chechnya. Economists estimate that Russia spent $5.5 billion on the war, causing annual budget deficits close to 10% of Russian GDP.

At the time of the Asian Financial Crisis, in 1998, Russia was dependent upon commodity exports, in particular, oil and gas. The crisis led to a sharp drop in commodity prices, which affected Russia's export revenue. This created further problems, because of Russia's large external debt caused by the war.

In 1997, the Russian ruble was pegged on a "floating band" at 5 to 6 rubles to the dollar.

On September 2, 1998, the Russian central bank abandoned the dollar peg, and allowed the ruble to float freely. By September 21, the exchange rate fell to 21 rubles for one US dollar. In other words, the Russian ruble lost 75% of its value.

As in Thailand, the price of imported goods surged. The cost of a dollar was now four times more expensive, in ruble terms. Imported jeans and electronics were now out reach for the average Russian.

Fortunately, the drop in the value of the currency was not catastrophic to Russia. This is because the Russian standard of living was already very low. Few people consumed imported goods. Other necessities were readily available. Russia had a long history of subsidizing bread production. In addition, many people supplemented their diet with vegetable gardens. Thus, people had food to eat. Few people owned automobiles. Since Russia was an oil producer, the country had plenty of heating fuel to get through the crisis.

The Russian experience demonstrates the importance of not being reliant upon imports, to survive a currency crisis.

Argentina -- 2001

The next country to fall was Argentina.

For much of the 1990s, Argentina experienced strong growth and low inflation. This growth was fueled by a large foreign debt. In 1995, Argentina's external debt was $99 billion –about 38% of the nation's GDP. By 2001, Argentina's foreign debt was more than half of the nation's GDP.

The Asian Financial Crisis caused Argentina's export earnings to drop. The slowdown was made worse in 1998, when Brazil devalued its currency. This made Brazilian exports much cheaper than those from Argentina – leading to a sharp reduction in Argentine exports. As a result, Argentina's trade deficit rose, and the country went into recession.

By 2001, the Argentina was in serious trouble. The nation began to experience a run on its banks, as people sought hard currency. On December 1, 2001, the government announced a freeze on bank accounts. As a result, deposit holders could no longer access their savings. The restrictions led to widespread hardship, causing protests and riots.

On December 5, 2001, the International Monetary Fund cut off support for the Argentine economy. This meant that Argentina could no longer service its large foreign debt. The country defaulted on $100 billion of foreign loans. This was the largest sovereign default up to that time.

In January 2002, Argentina abandoned its fixed exchange rate, of 1 to 1, for the Argentine peso to the U.S. dollar. By June 2002, the rate fell to 3.85 pesos to the dollar. This was a drop of 74% in the value of the peso.

By December of 2002, the Argentine economy had contracted by 20%, from the onset of the recession in 1998. Large numbers of people were thrown into poverty. The percentage of those living in poverty rose sharply, from 26% in 1998 to 58% in 2002.

Zimbabwe -- 2007

Let's take a look at one last country, which experienced hyperinflation in the early 2000s. That country is Zimbabwe.

As we have seen, Britain colonized large parts of Africa in the early 20th century. One of these countries was Rhodesia, located north of South Africa in the southern portion of the continent.

Under British rule, European settlers – primarily from England – established farms and businesses in the colony. Rhodesia became prosperous exporting minerals, such as chromium and manganese.

In 1980 – after a long colonial war – the native African residents of Rhodesia took control of the government. They changed the name of the country to Zimbabwe.

Zimbabwe adopted a new currency, known as the Zimbabwean dollar. The initial exchange rate was set at "par" to the dollar, or one to one.

From 1991 to 1996, Zimbabwe's new leader, Robert Mugabe, implemented an economic reform program. Mugabe evicted white landowners, and gave their property to native Africans. Many of the beneficiaries of this program were loyalists of Mugabe, and had no experience in agriculture. As a result, many farms fell into disrepair.

From 1999 to 2009, food production in Zimbabwe fell by 45%. White residents of Zimbabwe began to flee the country, taking their capital with them. As a result, manufacturing activity in Zimbabwe began to decline. Manufacturing output fell by 29% in 2005, 26% in 2006 and 28% in 2007. The banking sector also collapsed, since Zimbabwe's new farmers could not afford to pay their loans.

In March 1999, the Zimbabwean dollar was pegged at 38 to the dollar, a 97% devaluation from the date of independence. The exchange rate did not last long. Mugabe funded his government by printing large numbers of Zimbabwean dollars. By July 2006, the currency was trading at more than one million Zimbabwean dollars to the U.S. dollar.

Things got worse in the next couple years, as the country experienced hyperinflation. At the height of the hyperinflation, in 2008, it is estimated that prices increased by over one billion percent per month.

In April 2009, the Zimbabwean dollar was worthless. The government stopped printing any currency, and relied on foreign currencies, such as the U.S. dollar. As of 2024, 80% of all transactions in Zimbabwe were conducted in U.S. dollars.

The United States is vulnerable.

The examples of Thailand, Russia, Argentina and Zimbabwe show that the effects of a falling currency can be devastating for a country. Overnight, an entire nation can be plunged into poverty.

The United States is uniquely vulnerable to a currency collapse. The above countries had a low standard of living when their currency fell. The United States, on the other hand, has been rich for the past century. Our nation's infrastructure is premised upon cheap oil, and imported goods filling our malls.

If you are American, think of where you live. Chances are you live somewhere close to a highway exit that has a gas station, grocery store and possibly some "big box" stores such as Lowes or Home Depot. If the U.S. dollar were to collapse, the infrastructure at that highway exit will not produce any wealth at all. It is designed to consume the world's goods. You could easily be facing a shortage situation.

As we have seen, 70% of the U.S. economy is consumption. If we cannot afford imported goods, then 70% of our economy could rapidly disappear. If there are no imported goods in our malls, then there is no need to pay the store clerks, truck drivers, and marketing people to transport and sell those goods.

If the trade flows reverse, America could easily find itself living as people do in present-day Lebanon – living a life of poverty.

Our nation's automobile culture is particularly at risk. As we have seen, America doesn't actually manufacture cars. We assemble cars from imported parts. If the United States cannot afford parts imported from Mexico or Canada, then America could be without new cars for a time, at least until we set up factories to replace the imported parts.

America's reliance on imported oil is particularly concerning.

The United States imports one-third of the oil that it consumes.

According to the U.S. Energy Information Agency (EIA), the United States consumes about 20.6 million barrels of oil per day.

In May 2025, the United States produced just 13.5 million barrels of oil per day. That leaves a gap of 7.1 million barrels of oil per day, that must be imported.

America's oil production could, possibly, get much worse. As recently as 2008, the United States imported two-thirds of our nation's oil consumption.

In 2008, the United States started using a new technology, called "fracking" to get more oil out of the ground. Fracking injects water and chemicals at high pressures into the ground, to force open rock, to flush out more oil and natural gas. Between 2009 and 2019, fracking doubled our nation's production of oil and natural gas.

However, fracking may not be a permanent solution to our energy problems. Wells that are revitalized by fracking are typically 90% depleted within 36 months. In other words, after three years, fracking is no longer a solution. The well is worn out. When this happens, we have to drill another well, just to replace the prior production. As a result, the United States struggles to maintain its current production of crude oil.

Experts are debating whether the United States is about to see falling oil production, as we did in the early 1970s. Between 1970 and

2008, U.S. oil production fell by about half, due to the depletion of wells. In 1970, U.S. crude production peaked at 9.6 million barrels per day. By 2008, we were producing only about 5 million barrels per day. If the United States experiences declining oil production again, we could easily be forced to import more than half of our crude oil needs.

As we have seen, the United States imports over 7 million barrels per day of crude oil. More than half of this oil – 52% – comes from Canada. 11% is from Mexico; 5% from Saudi Arabia; and 4% from Iraq. These nations need to be paid. If this oil trades in a currency other than the U.S. dollar, then the United States will suffer a balance of payments crisis, due to our inability to pay for their oil.

The United States will face a national emergency, if we can't get this oil. Our nation's infrastructure – and our way of life – is dependent upon cheap oil.

Think again about where you live. If you live in the United States, statistically, you likely live in a suburban location. Most of us need cheap oil to get to and from work, to the grocery store, to take our kids to school, to mow our lawn, and to go to the shopping mall on the weekend. If that cheap oil disappears, you can kiss more than your barbecue grill goodbye.

Let's take a look at some numbers, and see what kind of balance of payments crisis the United States is facing.

As of August 2025, oil trades for about $66 a barrel. The United States needs 7.1 million barrels of oil per day, to cover the crude oil that our nation cannot produce. That means that the United States needs to come up with $469 million dollars every day, to import oil, to sustain our consumer society. That's $171 billion every year, or about one-fifth of our annual trade deficit.

But wait – you may say – the media is constantly telling us that the United States is "energy self-sufficient." Doesn't this mean that the United States has enough crude oil, to make gasoline for our consumer society?

The answer is no. The United States does not produce enough crude oil for our needs. We are producing, instead, natural gas. Natural gas cannot easily be converted into gasoline. While we can and do export much of that surplus natural gas, those exports are not sufficient to pay for our imported oil.

Now, for the scary part.

In a balance of payments crisis, a nation's currency tends to collapse. In Russia, Argentina and Thailand, the currency fell by 75%. In Lebanon, the lira fell by over 95%.

If the U.S. dollar falls 80%, the effect on the United States will be catastrophic. If that happens, then it will take five U.S. dollars – after the devaluation – to purchase the same amount of foreign goods as prior to the collapse.

In other words, the price of goods imported to the United States will rise 500%.

Think of what that means to your way of life. If gasoline were to double overnight, then the average price of gasoline in our country would be over $7 per gallon. If gasoline were to triple, then the price of that trip to the mall would cost you over $10 per gallon. And that's not even a 500% increase.

Most Americans would not be able to afford their daily commute, or be able to get a gallon of milk at the store. If the currency collapses, there won't be much demand at Walmart, Home Depot, or the scores of restaurants that dot the American landscape. Americans will be too busy trying to find hard currency, to pay for basic food imports.

At some price, the trucks will come off the road, at least for a period of time. When that happens, the shelves in Walmart will empty out, as we saw during the covid years. In a short period of time, our nation could be functioning as a barter society – if the government holds together at all.

The economics is pointing towards a major disaster, where 330 million people are without fuel and possibly, without food. And there are no safety rails in place. Remember, the Strategic Petroleum Reserve, put in place by the World War II generation, is half empty. We have no strategic grain reserve. Clinton, the child of 1950s prosperity, didn't think a grain reserve was necessary. We have few factories to manufacture goods to generate hard currency. Clinton, Obama and Biden didn't think factories were necessary.

As explained below, other areas are flashing warning signs to our nation.

CHAPTER 11
Premonitions of disaster

In October 1966, the Welsh coal mining town of Aberfan suffered a disaster that is still remembered in the United Kingdom. After days of rain, a pile of coal slurry slid down a hill into the town. The coal slurry engulfed a school and a row of houses, killing 116 children and 28 adults.

In London, a psychiatrist named John Barker had been studying premonitions reported by his patients. A premonition is a strong feeling that something is about to happen, especially something unpleasant. Barker wondered if the tragedy at Aberfan might have caused some people to have a premonition about the event.

Barker persuaded the newspaper in Aberfan to ask its readers if anyone had had a dream that might have foreseen the disaster. Barker received sixty letters in response. Of these, more than half claimed to have foreseen the disaster in a dream.

One of the letters was written by the parents of a ten-year-old girl who had died in the landslide. According to the letter, on the day before the event, the girl told her parents of a dream. In the dream, she tried to go to school, but there "was no school there." "Something black had come down over it." Another child, also killed in the landslide, had drawn a picture of a group of persons digging in a hillside. The caption on the drawing read, "the end."

Barker was impressed by the results. He decided to do a further experiment. He set up an organization called the London Premonition Bureau.

Barker asked the public to contact the Bureau if they had a dream of some impending disaster. He wanted to use the information from these reports to avert another tragedy.

Barker received numerous predictions at the Bureau. Over eighteen months, he received nearly one thousand reports of dreams allegedly predicting events. During 1968, one person repeatedly called and accurately predicted the assassination of Robert Kennedy. However, most tips were not helpful.

Two reports, however, were particularly intriguing. They claimed that the bureau's founder – John Barker – would soon die. Barker wasn't sure what to make of these reports. However, they proved to be true. On August 18, 1968, Barker died of a brain hemorrhage at age 44. Less than two years had passed since the landslide at Aberfan.

The London Premonitions Bureau stopped operating with his death.

Titanic Redux

The idea of seeing information, in advance, in a dream is known as precognition. There is no scientific evidence for precognition. According to scientists, precognition violates the principle of causation, because it suggests that something can be known in advance, before the event's causes come into existence. However, despite the lack of scientific evidence, precognition is widely reported and remains a topic of research and discussion.

For example, several people claim to have had premonitions of the Titanic sinking in 1912.

One such person was Morgan Robertson. In the late 1890s, Robertson had a vivid dream about the sinking of an ocean liner. "I could hear the screams of those who were stranded aboard her, and the helpless cries of those who were literally freezing to death in the water," he said. "I saw the name 'Titan' in the dream, and heard the word 'unsinkable,'" he reported.

Robertson wrote a book about the dream. It became known as the Wreck of the Titan. The book – published in 1898 – describes an ocean liner, called the Titan. Like the Titanic, the Titan was the largest and most modern ship of its day. Both the fictional Titan and the real-life Titanic were virtually the same size. Both ships were considered to be unsinkable, and both ships had an insufficient number of life boats. In Robertson's book, the Titan hits an iceberg during the month of April, and sinks. The actual Titanic sank fourteen years later, on April 14, 1912.

It's easy to dismiss Robertson's book as a coincidence, or the result of a writer with knowledge of shipbuilding and the dangers of the sea. However, other people claimed to have had similar dreams, predicting the disaster with Titanic. One such person was J. Connor Middleton. He described his dreams as follows:

> It may be of some interest to you to learn that on the 23rd March I booked my passage to New York on the White Star liner "TITANIC." About ten days before she sailed, I dreamt that I saw her floating on the sea, keel upwards, and her passengers and crew swimming around her.
>
> Although I am not given to dreaming at all; I was rather impressed with this dream, but I disclosed it to no one.... The following night, however, I had the very same dream, and I must admit, that I was somewhat uncomfortable about it.

Fortunately, for Middleton, his plans changed, and he cancelled his booking. This change saved his life. Before the ship sailed, Middleton told several people about his two dreams. These people later signed affidavits, stating that Middleton had told them about the dreams, predicting the disaster.

Esther Hart also claimed to have a premonition about the Titanic. Esther's husband, Benjamin, bought tickets for the entire family on the Titanic. After he did so, Esther had a premonition that the ship was going to sink. However, she was unable to convince her husband, Benjamin, to book passage on a different ship.

Shortly before sailing, Esther told Benjamin that she would not go to sleep on the vessel. She intended to sleep during the day, and stay awake every night on the Titanic. For four days, after the ship sailed, Esther went to bed in the morning, after breakfast. She then sat up, awake, every night – Wednesday, Thursday, Friday, and Saturday nights.

On Sunday evening, when the ship hit the iceberg, Esther quickly gathered her daughter, Eva, and went straight to the lifeboats. Esther and Eva survived the trip, and husband Benjamin died. Esther's daughter, Eva, described the premonition years later, in 1990, in a filmed interview. You can watch it on YouTube.

Esther Hart was not the only person who argued with her spouse about whether to sail on the Titanic. Frank Adelman had the same conversation with his wife, prior to sailing. Frank Adelman's wife had a premonition about the ship sinking. She urged her husband to change the booking. Frank agreed to flip a coin, to decide whether they should do so. The wife won the coin toss, and Frank changed the ticket. In late April 1912, the Adelmans returned home safely from Europe on a different ship, the Kaiser Wilhelm der Grosse. The couple's family and friends were astonished to learn that the Adelmans were alive, and had not gone down with the Titanic.

The events surrounding the sinking of the Titanic are not isolated. For example, consider this strange story involving President Abraham Lincoln. Shortly before his death, Lincoln told several people that he was having a recurring dream. In the dream, Lincoln walked through the White House, and found a room draped in black. In the center of the room, there was casket guarded by soldiers. When Lincoln asked who the dead person was, a soldier told him, "the President has been shot."

More recently, the events involving the World Trade Center, in New York, have led to claims of premonitions. These go back to the first bombing of the Twin Towers, in 1993.

On February 26, 1993, Wall Street executive, Barrett Naylor, was going to work at the World Trade Center, in New York. At Grand Central Station, in midtown Manhattan, Naylor had a strong feeling that he should not go to work that day. He turned around and went home. Naylor avoided the first bombing of the World Trade Center. Eight years later, on September 11, 2001, Naylor got the same feeling, and did not go to work. Naylor survived the collapse of the building on that day.

Naylor is not the only person who felt uncomfortable about going to work at the World Trade Center on the day of the attack. According to Bonnie McEneaney, her husband Eamon dreaded going to work at the WTC complex during the summer of 2001. Eamon described vivid nightmares of buildings collapsing and people trapped in fires. Eamon later died in the events of 911. After his death, Bonnie described these experiences in her book, Messages: Signs, Visits, and Premonitions from Loved Ones Lost on 9/11.

We also have reports of premonitions from events involving mass shootings.

On December 14, 2012, a gunman entered Sandy Hook Elementary School, in Newtown, Connecticut, and killed 20 children and 6 staff members. Two weeks prior to the shooting, five-year-old Logan Dyer had to be removed from class due to panic attacks. Logan's mother removed him from school due to his anxiety. When doctors recommended that Logan return to school, he would scream, "No, no! It's not a safe place. I am scared." Logan Dyer survived the shooting.

As we see from the above examples, premonitions – whether true or not – appear to be warnings of future danger. When the danger involves a large number of people – such as the Titanic disaster, the landslide in Wales, or the events of 911 – a greater number of people claim to have foreseen the event.

Premonitions of Economic Collapse

I first started hearing premonitions of economic collapse in the United States in 2005.

In that year, a friend told me that she was having a recurring dream about a "mob coming up her farm road to kill and eat the horses."

I was shocked. This woman had spent her entire life living in a safe and prosperous country – the United States. She was not a war victim. She didn't survive the battle of Berlin, or the famine in Ethiopia. It made no sense that my friend was having recurring dreams about famine and mob violence in the United States.

I began to wonder whether perhaps her dream was a premonition.

I soon encountered other people who claimed to have had similar dreams of economic collapse in the United States. Their reports were vivid and astonishing. A former girlfriend told me that she dreamt of refugees walking north through Virginia's Shenandoah Valley, with nothing to eat. A law partner told me that he had a dream of people fleeing the United States. A longtime restaurant owner reported dreams of famine and violence in America. "It's terrible, just terrible," he told me. "People could starve here." A woman from New York told me that she dreamt of people gathered on rooftops for safety.

With each account, my eyes grew wider. I wasn't sure what to make of these reports. Collectively, these dreams were like a jigsaw puzzle, where the pieces – astonishingly – fit together and created an image of the United States that was very different from today.

In 2012, I discovered that other people in the United States were saying similar things. These were people who had suffered a medical emergency, and claimed to have undergone a spiritual experience known as a "near-death experience."

Near-death experiences were first identified in 1975 by American psychiatrist, Raymond A. Moody. In his book, Life After Life, Moody found that people who are clinically dead – and later revived – tend to report similar experiences. According to Moody, these people reported the ability to observe events from a perspective outside of their body. Many experienced an intense feeling of love, a life review, and the ability to communicate with deceased love ones. Since 1975, hundreds of books have been written about Near Death Experiences (NDE), many by medical doctors. Thousands of people have described their experiences in interviews online.

Here's the interesting thing. Some of the NDE experiencers claim that they were shown a possible future of the United States, during their experience. Often, this involved a warning of economic collapse. This trend was so significant that the group that studies NDEs – the International Association for Near-Death Studies (IANDES) – presented a lecture on the subject at one of the group's annual conferences.

Let's take a look at what some of these people are saying.

In 2015, Hector Sosa, Jr. wrote a book called, A Change is Coming. In his book, Sosa describes a number of dreams or waking premonitions about the future of the United States. He says that the crisis will start with soaring gasoline prices:

> Just before the meltdown becomes fully evident, gasoline prices will soar. I've been having a recurring dream where I'm at different gas stations during this time. In the dream I'm in the process of filling my car when I look up and notice that prices start at $7 a gallon. I also saw prices between $7.00 and $7.65 for unleaded. Each dream is at a different

gas station. I sensed that people on a fixed income could hardly afford to drive. There were no semis on the street. At the Springville Maverick near I-15, I looked across the street at the Flying J Truck Stop. There were hardly any trucks parked there.

The store shelves will not be stocked, because the trucking industry will come to a halt. There will be no gasoline available, and neither will there be gas for cooking or heating homes.

In 2016, Sharon Milliman wrote a book about her own near-death experience. Most of her book, A Song in the Wind, is about love, a life review, and reunions with deceased family members. However, in one section, she provided a graphic warning about where events were leading in the United States. She wrote:

> I saw people being killed by bombings and shootings. I witnessed our financial institutions crumbling. In the end, our money was not worth the paper it was written on. In money's place, I was shown silver and gold coins being used to make purchases.

In 2002, Sarah Lenelle Menet, described her NDE in a book entitled, There is No Death. Menet claims that she, too, was shown a glimpse of a possible future for the United States. She describes covid-like lockdowns, where commerce briefly comes to a halt. After this event, she saw a horrific collapse of the United States:

> As the people were fleeing the cities in the hope of saving their lives, gangs were attacking and killing them. . . . There was chaos, with looting, rioting, and murders involved -- a complete breakdown of society. Many people seemed to have gone crazy. I sensed that the electricity had failed everywhere, and that nothing was operating throughout

> the country, including any communications systems. I watched people throw rocks through windows to steal TVs that would not work and thought it very strange.
>
> The economy and the electricity were completely gone. Chaos and anarchy reigned over the entire country because, without any governmental structure, there was a total breakdown. I saw people's hearts fail them from fear. Almost everyone was searching in a desperate attempt to find some food. There was an extreme shortage everywhere but in some areas there was no food at all. In these places, I could see people so hungry they were digging in the ground for worms.

Menet did provide a ray of hope, in her book. In her NDE, she was told that some communities would establish safe havens shortly before the collapse. She saw twenty or thirty safe havens, where people had stockpiled food and were safe. Most of these locations were in the western United States, with only about three locations in the East.

Hector Sosa also reported seeing safe havens in his book, A Change is Coming. Sosa had a dream about refugees fleeing the eastern United States, to the west. "Everybody looked disheveled.... They looked like they had been sleeping in the dirt," he wrote.

In 1985, Howard Storm, an American college professor, developed a severe case of peritonitis during a trip to Paris. Storm, who was an atheist at the time, claimed that he experienced a negative NDE, when he was briefly dead. He described the experience in a book entitled, My Descent into Death.

Storm, like the others, claims that he was shown a possible future of the United States. He was given the following warning:

> If the United States continues to exploit the rest of the world by greedily consuming the world's resources... your country will collapse economically, which will result in civil

chaos. Because of the greedy nature of people, you will have people killing people for a cup of gasoline. The world will watch in horror as your country is obliterated by strife. The rest of the world will not intervene because they have been victims of your exploitation. They will welcome the annihilation of such selfish people.

Storm later became a minister in Ohio. However, he spends time in Belize, where he periodically does mission work.

Some people dismiss near death experiences as unusual dreams of a dying mind. However, it is possible to verify certain parts of the NDE experience. Many people who experience NDEs claim to have a perspective that is outside of their body, during their dying moments. In other words, when the doctors are working to resuscitate their body, the patient claims to be in the room, observing the situation from over the doctor's shoulder, or from some upper corner of the room.

These patients report – with astonishing accuracy – what happened in the room, and what was said in the room while they were clinically brain dead. They can report what the room looked like, even though they never saw the operating room. This sort of information is known as "veridical" information. It is called veridical because it can used to verify the dying patient's observations of events that occurred when they were clinically dead.

IANDES, the group which studies NDEs, has tracked accounts of veridical information for nearly half a century. IANDES has published a book which includes over 130 accounts of NDEs which can be verified by doctors, nurses or other persons in the vicinity of the dying person. The title of the book is The Soul Does Not Die.

Increasingly, science is starting to take near-death experiences seriously, as a legitimate topic of study. The existence of veridical information moves the topic to the realm of the scientific method, because we are now dealing with information that can be verified.

More than one hundred scientific journals have published articles about near-death experiences.

Whether one chooses to believe these accounts is up to the individual. I offer these accounts only to provide an alternative perspective. While spirituality can be debated, the laws of economics cannot be denied. According to the laws of mathematics, the U.S. dollar is unstable, and could potentially collapse.

CHAPTER 12
Solutions

The United States government appears to have been blissfully unaware of the dangers of the petrodollar, until recently.

Former President Joseph Biden appeared to have no understanding of the role Saudi Arabia plays in sustaining the petrodollar. During the 2020 presidential campaign, Biden criticized Saudi Arabia's human rights record. He promised to make Saudi Crown Prince, Mohammed bin Salman, a "pariah" on the world stage, due to the prince's alleged involvement in the murder of a journalist, Jamal Khashoggi.

Biden pledged to reassess the U.S.-Saudi security relationship. After being sworn-in as president, Biden began to undermine Saudi security in the Middle East. In 2021, Saudi Arabia was fighting a war with Houthi rebels, located in Yemen. Biden refused to designate the rebels as "terrorists" under American law, upsetting Saudi Arabia's leaders. Biden also refused to sell certain weapons to the Saudis. These moves raised questions as to whether the Biden administration was committed to defending the kingdom.

The Saudis responded to Biden's criticism by making it clear that they could sell oil for currencies other than the dollar. They also made it clear that they could purchase weapons from someplace other than the United States. As of 2021, Saudi Arabia was the largest overseas customer for American arms. Biden quickly changed his tune.

On July 15, 2022, President Biden traveled to Saudi Arabia, and met with Prince Mohammed bin Salman. This was not the warmest visit. Biden refused to shake hands with Mohammed bin Salman, and insisted on only doing a "fist bump," allegedly due to the covid situation.

Shortly thereafter, the United States announced that it was considering a formal alliance with Saudi Arabia, to provide military support for the nation. Some compared the proposed deal to NATO. It was whispered that the United States was considering selling civilian nuclear technology to the Saudis. Unmentioned, was the implied term that Saudi Arabia would continue to maintain the petrodollar monopoly.

The U.S.-Saudi deal got hung up on the status of Israel. The United States insisted that Saudi Arabia normalize its relationship with Israel, as part of the deal. This was important, from the American point of view, due to the proposed transfer of nuclear technology to the kingdom. Saudi Arabia refused to accept this term, without protection for the Palestinian people.

On October 7, 2023, the deal was put on hold, after Hamas-led militants attacked Israel from the Gaza Strip. The ensuing war between Israel and Hamas made it diplomatically difficult for Saudi Arabia to recognize Israel.

President Trump has been much more attuned to the importance of the petrodollar. In 2017, Trump made his first overseas trip to Saudi Arabia. Trump was the first U.S. president to go to Saudi Arabia for his initial official trip.

Saudi Arabia rolled out the red carpet for Trump. American and Saudi flags lined the highways of Riyadh, and billboards showed pictures of Trump. Jets flew overhead, with red, white and blue contrails. During the visit, Trump signed an arms deal with Saudi Arabia worth $350 billion, over 10 years.

SOLUTIONS

Following his re-election, Trump again went to Saudi Arabia for his first overseas trip. In May 2025, Trump visited Saudi Arabia, Qatar, and the United Arab Emirates – all key players for the petrodollar. During the visit, Trump announced that Saudi Arabia had agreed to invest $600 billion in the United States. This included Saudi Arabia's purchase of $142 billion of American-made weapons – the largest arms deal in history.

There was no public announcement as to whether Saudi Arabia would continue to sell oil only for U.S. dollars. However, we can be certain that Trump raised the issue. Trump has repeatedly emphasized the importance of using the U.S. dollar in world trade.

This is reasonable point of view. The oil monopoly allows the United States to print trillions of dollars, and convert such money to gold. The monopoly allows the United States to place armies throughout the Middle East, and brings untold wealth to our shores. However, like all monopolies, the petrodollar is unstable.

If the BRICS alliance adopts a new currency – and prices commodities in the new BRICS currency – the U.S. dollar could collapse overnight. Our leaders need to read the writing on the wall, and mitigate a foreseeable decline in the dollar.

The United States needs to reach out to other nations to negotiate this transition. China, being stronger than the United States, is the natural place to look. There are indications that China does not want to blow up the U.S. market, by allowing the dollar to collapse. China has benefitted from the American market for a generation. It does not want this cash flow to come to a sudden end.

Sixty years ago, Britain found itself in a similar situation, with the decline of the British pound. It is useful to review the British experience, for ideas in dealing with a currency's decline.

Lessons from the British pound.

In the 19th century, Britain had the largest economy in the world. Britain controlled a quarter of the globe, and ran much of the world. Britain's position was not unlike that of the United States today.

However, times change. By 1913, the United States was the world's leading commercial power. At the end of World War I, in 1918, the United States was the world's leading creditor nation. Gold was piling up in New York, rather than London. All of this put pressure on the British pound, as the world's leading reserve currency.

In 1950, the world's central banks held nearly 58% of their foreign currency reserves in British pounds. By 1977, this number was only 2%. Britain achieved this decline in a peaceful manner, unnoticed by anyone other than a few bankers.

However, the transition was not easy. Economist Catherine Schenk argues that Britain actively managed the decline of its currency over a twenty year period. Britain did this in two ways.

1) Britain worked with its trading partners to obtain lines of credit, to ensure the liquidity of the British pound.

2) Britain worked with its former colonies to encourage them to hold as many British pounds as possible, to create demand for the currency.

According to Schenk, by the late 1940s, it became apparent that the pound could no longer be used as the world's reserve currency. By then, Britain's ratio of gold and foreign currency to pound liabilities was greater than 4 to 1. This led to concerns of a possible run on the pound.

To reduce the risk of a currency collapse, Britain worked with the world's economic leaders to cushion the foreseeable decline in the value of the pound.

In 1963 and 1964, Britain negotiated lines of credit to cover short-term speculative attacks on the pound. These lines of credit bought time to look for a long-term solution to the international community's diversification of foreign exchange reserves away from the pound.

In 1966, Britain entered into an agreement with the Bank of International Settlements (BIS). Under the agreement, BIS agreed to finance 50% of any major demand on the British pound. Britain sought to reassure the international community that it would have sufficient funds to repurchase pounds from overseas, to avoid a run on the currency.

The arrangement was not entirely successful. In November 1967, Britain was forced to devalue the pound by 14.3%, due to a chronic balance of payments problem. The devaluation made the cost of imports more expensive, in terms of pounds, correcting the imbalance. More importantly, the devaluation reduced pressure on the pound, by bringing its value closer to fair market value.

In March 1968, Britain obtained an additional $4 billion credit facility from the IMF, to provide standby support for the pound. This would be the equivalent of $34 billion today.

In 1968, Britain entered into the Basle Agreement with the central banks of the G10 countries. The agreement set up an additional $2 billion line-of-credit, worth $17 billion today. Britain could draw on the line-of-credit if the Bank of England's reserves fell to less than £3 billion.

As a condition for the credit, the G10 banks insisted that Britain encourage other nations to hold their reserves in British pounds. Between July and September 1968, Britain entered into agreements with 34 countries holding sterling. These agreements became known as Sterling Agreements.

The United States, Canada, Germany and France did not agree to enter into a Sterling Agreement. Instead, all 34 countries were either present or former British colonies. Many of the colonies were not happy about agreeing to hold British pounds, due to the 14% devaluation of the pound in 1967.

To sweeten the deal, Britain agreed to guarantee 90% of the value of each country's holdings of British pounds, in the event the value of the pound fell, against the value of other major currencies. Countries entering into a Sterling Agreement could diversify their reserves, and sell pounds sterling. However, if they did so, Britain would no longer guarantee the value of their pound holdings.

A chart showing the percentage of sterling that each country agreed to hold is set forth below.

Table 12.1

1968 Sterling Agreements
Minimum Sterling Percentages for
Official Reserves

County	Percent
East Caribbean Currency Authority	100
Gambia	100
Hong Kong	99
Barbados	97
Mauritius	95
British Hondura	90
Bahamas	80
Bermuda	80
Ceylon	80
Ghana	80
Guyana	80
Malawi	80

Trinidad	80
Malta	75
Bahrain	70
New Zealand	70
Sierra Leone	70
Zambia	65
Nigeria	60
Jamaica	57
Ireland	55
Uganda	51
Cyprus	50
Dubai	50
Iceland	45
Malaysia	40
Australia	40
Pakistan	40
Singapore	40
Jordan	25
Tanzania	25
Kuwait	25
Libya	18
India	13

As indicated above, the Sterling Agreements required the participating countries to hold between 13% and 100% of their foreign currency reserves in British pounds. India, which had a highly-adversarial relationship with the UK, agreed to hold only 13% of its reserves in pounds. Meanwhile, Hong Kong, which remained under British control in 1968, agreed to hold virtually all of its reserves in pounds.

Britain renewed most of the agreements in 1971, 1973 and 1974. With each renewal, Britain agreed to reduce the required percentage of pounds sterling by 10%.

The Sterling Agreements delayed the world's diversification of currency reserves, away from the British pound. The following chart shows the rapid reduction in sterling held by other countries during this period, versus the Sterling Agreement countries.

Table 12.2

Percentage British pounds in foreign exchange reserves

Year	Sterling Agreement Countries	All Countries
1968	57.9	20
1969	56.1	17.5
1970	53.7	5.2
1971	61.6	4.5
1972	54.5	4.7

As indicated by the above chart, countries that did not participate in the Sterling Agreements reduced their holdings of British pounds from an average of 20% of their reserves in 1968, to just 4.7% five years later, in 1972. Meanwhile, the Sterling group countries continued to hold over fifty percent of their foreign currency reserves in British pounds, as of 1972. This is an important precedent, for reducing the world's reliance on U.S. dollars, in light of a new BRICS currency.

Between 1968 and 1972, the British pound continued to decline against the dollar. Britain was required to pay two rounds of compensation to the participants, in October 1972 and October 1973. The agreements expired at the end of 1974.

In the end, Britain was successful, in avoiding a collapse of its currency. As of 1976, few countries held significant reserves in British pounds. Only 20 countries held more than ten million pounds, and only New Zealand had more than 50% of its reserves in sterling.

When the oil market rejected the British pound in December 1974, Britain was able to survive the foreseeable drop in demand for its currency. Britain had emergency stand-by credit facilities in place, and was prepared.

Lessons for the United States.

When Britain sounded the alarm on a potential currency collapse, Britain's foreign debt was four times greater than the country's reserve assets – consisting primarily of gold and U.S. dollars. Economists refer this concept as "overhang."

Overhang exists where there is a large supply of a particular asset, such as shares of stock, that is likely to be sold, and could potentially put downward pressure on the asset's price.

By continuing to run budget deficits, the federal government is creating a situation where there is a large overhang of U.S. Treasury bonds. As of July 2025, the United States has a cumulative national debt of $37 trillion. Most of this debt is reflected in the Treasury bond market.

Due to the trade deficit, the United States has few foreign currency reserves, to deal with the overhang of U.S. Treasury bonds. The United States holds less than $1 trillion of gold. Thus, we are looking at an overhang of Treasury bonds to foreign reserves, of about 37 to 1. That makes the American problem about eight times greater than the problem faced by Britain in 1961.

Several economists have suggested that the United States work with its trading partners to devalue the dollar, by means of an agreement similar to the Plaza Accord, implemented in 1985. These economists have suggested calling the accord a Mar-a-Lago Accord, named after President Trump's resort in Florida, where such an agreement could be negotiated.

If the United States does not voluntarily devalue the dollar, by means of a Mar-a-Lago Accord, or otherwise, then the world will eventually lose faith in the dollar. When this happens, the overhang will force the value of the dollar down, potentially catastrophically.

National Goals

In addition to learning from Britain, the United States needs to take a page from China's playbook. Since 1953, China has used Five Year Plans to set national goals. After seventy-five years, these national goals are starting to pay major dividends for the Chinese people. During this time, China's leaders have lifted hundreds of millions of people from poverty, to lives approaching middle class standards.

For many years, the United States has been adverse to setting national goals. Economists claimed that the government should stay out of the private market, and refrain from picking winners and losers. However, history has shown that an economy will not develop, unless government intervenes to do so. We have seen how our nation promoted our textile industry in the early 1800s, by means of protective tariffs. Our national government also promoted railroads in the 19th century by subsidizing their construction. We also promoted the passenger car, by building the interstate highway system in the 20th century.

Whenever the United States has used national goals, our nation has achieved extraordinary accomplishments. For ten years, during the 1960s, the United States pursued the goal of sending a man to the moon, and bringing him safely back to earth. The Apollo program was successful, and led to many benefits for America, as the program pushed our nation ahead technologically. We saw similar benefits from the national goal of winning World War II in the 1940s.

Jim Rohn, a motivational speaker, used to tell his listeners that they should set a goal of becoming a millionaire. Rohn would tell his audience not to do this for the money. Instead, he told them, you should set a goal of becoming a millionaire because it will force you to become a stronger person. The same is true with a nation.

For example, suppose the United States set a goal of achieving a $100 billion trade surplus in automobiles. This single goal would completely change the future of the United States, and make the nation much stronger.

In 2024, the United States ran a trade deficit of $205 billion in the sale of vehicles. To reverse this loss, and create a profit for the nation, the United States would have to devalue its currency, to make its autos competitive with those sold by Japan, Germany, Mexico and China. If the United States devalued its currency in a controlled manner – preferably in cooperation with other countries – the United States would substantially boost its manufacturing ability. Factories would return to the United States, because it would be cost effective to make goods in our nation once again.

And that's just one goal. China has been setting goals since 1953. It is time for the United States to follow their lead, and chart a course to a better future.

CHAPTER 13
How to Protect Your Family

The first rule of self-defense is situational awareness.

In other words, if you are walking down a dark street at night, you should look into dark alleys before walking past them. If you are in a deserted park, and see a dangerous figure in the distance, you should pay attention that person, and if necessary, avoid them. This is situational awareness, and it's the first rule of self-defense.

Situational awareness also applies on a national basis. If there are riots down the street, you stay away from the riots, if you are smart. If your currency is in danger of collapse – due to half a century of trade deficits – then you should think through the consequences of a currency collapse, and how this could affect your family. This book has tried to raise awareness of the risk of the U.S. dollar falling in value quickly, and the danger such a collapse poses to our communities.

You now know that the dollar is artificially sustained by the reserve currency, and could lose a portion of its buying power in the future. How can you best protect your family, and your assets, if the dollar were to collapse?

Fortunately, there is no need to reinvent the wheel on this question. As we have seen, many other countries have experienced a sudden, material drop in the value of their currency. We have looked at Thailand, Lebanon, Russia, Argentina and Zimbabwe.

Argentina, for example, has many lessons that we can learn.

As we have seen, Argentina's currency fell 74% in early 2002. At that point, no one wanted to accept paper money. The country went to a barter economy for next eighteen months. In a barter economy, people trade goods or services of tangible value, in return for similar items.

During this time, Argentina became a more dangerous place. Riots occurred, and home invasions increased. Homes in isolated locations were more dangerous, because they didn't have the protection of neighbors.

In Argentina, some people knew in advance that the currency collapse was coming. Wealthy families prepared in advance. They purchased homes across the border, in Paraguay, Uruguay or Chile. When things got difficult, these families simply crossed the border, and remained safe until things calmed down.

Let's consider each of these lessons, one at a time, and see what we can do in the United States, to prepare for a currency collapse.

Barter items

Think about all the things that you use that are imported. In the United States, that is pretty much everything. It includes our cell phones, laptop computers, printers, dishes, coffee makers, lamps, power tools, clothing, jeans, and shoes. If the U.S. dollar fell 50%, then the price of these items will double overnight. If the dollar were to fall 75%, then the price of these items will increase by 400% overnight. Think about that. The cell phone that formerly cost you $700 would now cost $2,800 of America's much less valuable dollars.

Keep your guns in a safe location – preferably locked – and away from children. If you have children in the house, store your guns in a locked safe. And if you are remotely depressed, then do not keep a gun in the house.

If the United States faces a currency collapse, work with your neighbors to ensure the security of your neighborhood. Here in Tennessee, the prepping community knows who their friends are, and what they can expect if things were to fall apart.

Remote real estate in the United States

The second rule of self-defense is tactical relocation.

In other words, if you see a potential danger on the street, you should take steps to avoid the danger. If you are in a battle, and your position is being overrun, it is often better to defend the front line from a more secure position, if authorized to do so. This is known as tactical relocation. It is rule number two of self-defense.

In the early 1990s, an American military officer – John Wesley Rawles – wrote a novel about a group of people who stockpiled food, guns and supplies at a remote location in the United States, in anticipation of a currency collapse. The novel, entitled Patriots: A Novel of Survival in the Coming Collapse, tells how this group of people fought to survive, after the economy fell apart.

It is interesting that Rawles saw the dangers with the dollar thirty years ago, in the early 1990s. Unfortunately, the risks that he identified are still with us today.

I live in Knoxville, Tennessee. After the covid years, hundreds of thousands of people moved to Eastern Tennessee, to escape life in the larger cities. Many of these people have told me that they moved to Knoxville to be in a safer location, if economic conditions deteriorate. Many bought large plots of land, at some distance from the city.

Their moves are not unlike the trends that we saw in the early 1970s, when there was a back-to-basics movement in the United States. At that time, many younger people moved to remote locations, and sought to live a self-sufficient lifestyle. They purchased remote cabins, grew their own food, and gathered eggs from chickens. They were driven by the perceived romance of communes, as dramatized in movies like Easy Rider, and by books such as the Foxfire series, about self-sufficiency.

Today's preppers are largely hidden from view. They are quietly making plans, in case things fall apart. For example, a colonel in the U.S. Army, who works in Virginia, recently purchased 180 acres of land on a mountain top in northeastern Tennessee. The property is miles from the nearest city. I doubt this sophisticated officer would have bought property on a remote mountaintop in Tennessee, if our nation had its financial house in order.

I don't recommend selling all of your possessions, and moving to a mountain top. I do recommend having a conversation with like-minded friends or relatives, and knowing where you would be safe, if you had to tactically relocate. Have a tent and camping equipment available, in case you need to retreat to a safer location. Remember, rich nation, strong army. The opposite is also true. Poverty attracts civil violence, riots, and possible warfare.

Stockpiling food

It's important to recognize that you can't eat your bullets. If the price of gasoline doubles overnight, we must be ready for the possibility that food may not be available for a period of time. The trucks could come off the road.

During the covid years – from March 2020 to about March 2022 – we saw how quickly stores shelves can empty out. At the beginning of the epidemic, certain items – such as toilet paper – quickly disappeared from Walmart. Later in the crisis, in early 2022, the ports were jammed, making it impossible for some items to get into the country. Large parts of Walmart's shelves were empty for a period of time, as a result.

Should you stockpile food, and if so, how much?

It is interesting to consider the Mormons' policy on stockpiling food. The Church of Latter Day Saints recommends having a three-month supply of food, at any given time. The Mormons are not prepping for doomsday. They recommend storing food to develop self-reliance. The church's recommendation is borne from hard experience. Many of these families are descendants of settlers who came to the western United States in the 19th century.

I recommend having at least five months of food stockpiled, at least until the United States sorts matters out regarding the reserve currency. This is easier than it may sound. Canned goods are typically good for a few years. I recommend keeping a few bags of rice and flour available.

Dried foods are also an interesting option. For example, Augason Farms makes a powdered black bean burger. The product has a shelf life of up to twenty-five years. This is a great way to get protein, if the trucks are off the road. It only takes a few minutes to create the burger patty by adding warm water; and the burger tastes surprisingly like real beef. Powdered eggs and powdered mash potatoes are other options, with long shelf lives.

Knowing how to bake bread is also a useful skill. During the covid epidemic, bread quickly disappeared from store shelves in some areas. As always, keep an eye on expiration dates.

If you live in a rural location, or have a yard, you may want to invest in a home vegetable garden, at least until the currency adjusts. Our parents' generation considered a home garden to be a necessity. They also knew how to can their own food. As always, be reasonable, and keep it fun.

Prepper conventions and podcasts

Now that you have some idea where to go, in the event of problems, it is time to make your remote location a bit more comfortable, and secure.

If you had to get water from a stream or from a well, do you know how to purify the water? Do you have a container for transporting and storing water? Do you have a generator or solar cells for producing electricity, if the lights go out? Do you have night-vision goggles, to check the perimeter at night?

I am not saying that you need any of these things. However, a lot of preppers consider these types of items to be essential.

The best way to get information about prepping goods and services is by means of prepper podcasts, YouTube channels, or a prepper convention. Since the covid years, there has been an explosion of interest in the United States in self-reliance. This has been reflected in the number of podcasts, internet channels, and conventions dedicated to the prepping community.

Some of the top prepping shows online are the Casual Preppers Podcast, the Fieldcraft Survival Podcast, the Survival Show, and the Bear Independent Podcast. These are just a few of more than a dozen podcasts and YouTube channels dedicated to getting Americans ready for possible problems in the United States.

Major media outlets are starting to jump onboard. The History Channel produces a reality show, called Alone, where participants compete to be the last one standing in the wilderness. Even National Geographic has a show called Doomsday Preppers, dedicated to the subject.

Similarly, it is now possible to find a prepper convention in virtually every state. These include the Great Lakes Emergency Preparedness Expo; the Boulder Prepper Show; the Minnesota Prepping Expo; and the Thrivalist Fair, in Washington State. Not all of these shows are in remote locations. For example, Los Angeles, California has an annual

"Survival Convention," and Long Beach, California has an event called "Ready Long Beach."

Precious metals

Now that we have taken a look at immediate safety, it's time to consider protecting one's assets. Kyle Bass's idea of buying gold is a good one. Smart people have used gold as a store of value for thousands of years. The gold excavated from King Tut's tomb in 1922 had the same value – in terms of real purchasing power – that it had when it was placed in the tomb three thousand years earlier.

The modern kings of finance are aware of the dollar's weakness, and are stockpiling gold at a record pace. These kings are the world's central bankers. In 2024, the world's central banks collectively purchased over a thousand tons of gold. 2025 will be the fourth year of large gold purchases by the banks. According to gold consultant, Metals Focus, the banks are diversifying their investments. They are selling dollar-denominated assets, and converting the proceeds into gold.

This buying has put upward pressure on the value of gold. As recently as 2018, you could purchase an ounce of gold for as little as $1,200. The price is triple that today.

Wealthy Americans are taking their cue from the world's investment banks. In recent years, purchases of physical gold in the United States have gone through the roof. We first saw this trend during covid. In April and May of 2020, gold imports to the United States tripled. In 2025, with the threat of tariffs looming, our nation's gold merchants pulled out the stops. In the first two months of 2025, the United States imported over 600 tons of gold. This stockpile, worth about $64 billion, is more than 10% of all of the gold in Fort Knox. Some very wealthy people are stocking up.

Gold is not an ideal barter item. Gold is too expensive to exchange for common every-day items. However, gold is an important hedge against inflation and a falling dollar. If the stock market takes a hit, due to a falling dollar, then gold can be an important way to preserve family wealth, provided that it is stored in a physically-secure location.

For many years, countries have stored their gold in remote locations on the planet, deemed to be safe from warfare. Wealthy individuals are doing the same thing. Certain services will allow you to store gold in Switzerland, London or Singapore. Thus, if things fall apart in the United States, you don't have to worry. Your gold is out of the country. Your gold will also be protected from government confiscation, as happened in our nation in 1933.

However, storing gold outside of the United States is an expensive way to protect your assets. Unlike a share of stock, gold does not pay a dividend. Gold earns no return, other than generally keeping up with inflation. In addition, if you opt for third party storage, expect to pay a fee for the cost of their vault. If you choose to keep gold on your property, put it someplace safe. Keep it locked up, and have it ready to go, if you have to retreat to a safer location.

If you want precious metals that are tradable, then you need to consider silver. At about $39 an ounce, silver is ideal for smaller economic transactions.

It is possible to buy silver "rounds," weighing an ounce or two. Silver rounds are minted by private mints, and come in a variety of designs. They are clearly marked with their weight in silver. As of August 2025, a silver round weighing an ounce sells for about $42 – about the cost of a tank of gas.

Some people prefer old silver dollars, or other U.S.-minted silver coins. Silver dollars issued before 1965 were 90% silver, and 10% copper. As a result, these coins have maintained their value over the years. As of 2025, old silver dollars sell for about $37, for their scrap value. If the coin is a rare year, or in good condition, then the price can be significantly higher.

Old silver dollars are a wonderful hedge against inflation. They are also a lot of fun. However, keep in mind that the numismatic value of the coin may fall in an economically stressful situation. Thus, I would recommend keeping an eye on the premium paid for the coin, over the market value of the coin's silver content.

Bitcoin and crypto currency.

Many people recommend investing in bitcoin or crypto currency, as a means to diversify out of the U.S. dollar. I don't recommend doing so.

Let's look at a bit of history, to explain.

In the 16th century, Dutch merchants imported tulip bulbs from the Ottoman Empire. At that time, tulip bulbs were rare. They produced pretty plants, and became a symbol of wealth and status. In 1634, people began to trade tulip bulbs like stocks. Between 1634 and 1637, prices of tulip bulbs rose to exorbitant levels, with some bulbs selling for the price of a house. This period became known as "Tulip Mania." The bubble burst in February 1637, when prices plummeted. Many individuals faced financial ruin. I view bitcoin and crypto currency as, essentially, a tulip bulb.

Yes, bitcoin has gone from nearly zero to over $100,000 since 2013. And yes, bitcoin has a limited supply, which keeps demand high.

However, bitcoin has no intrinsic value. You are essentially buying air. This is reflected in the large price swings that we see in bitcoin, and other crypto currencies. In the event of a national emergency, bitcoin will likely be of little assistance to you. If the power is out, bitcoin will not do you any good at all. It would be better to own a can of beans, a bag of rice, a flashlight, or perhaps, an edible tulip bulb.

Domestic foreign currency accounts.

In countries that experienced a currency collapse, the population quickly learned to do business in stronger currencies. In other words, if Lebanese lira was worthless, then people traded goods in euro or U.S.

dollars. This can be a good way to protect value, if you can access the stronger currency.

In the United States, it is not easy to obtain currencies other than the U.S. dollar. Many banks will sell currency issued by other countries, typically for a vacation. However, buying currency from a bank can be expensive, with high transaction costs. In addition, in the event of a crisis, your neighbors will not likely be interested in paper notes from Canada or the EU, even though such currencies may retain their value.

Thus, if you intend to purchase foreign currency, you should do so only as a currency play, to diversify your investments.

Very few banks in the United States provide accounts denominated in foreign currencies. One of the few is Everbank. Everbank allows its depositors to set up accounts in a variety of foreign currencies. These include the euro, the British pound, the Swiss franc, and the Japanese yen. Everbank also has accounts for certain emerging market currencies, such as the Chinese yuan, the Brazilian real, the Czech koruna, and the Mexican peso.

Having $10,000 or $30,000 worth of a foreign currency can be a comforting thing. If the dollar drops, you theoretically have preserved some value, for potential use later.

However, investment in foreign currency has its drawbacks. You are only purchasing a currency, and not a productive asset. The money sits in the bank at a low rate of interest, if any. Thus, after inflation, you may not get much of a return.

In addition, the exchange rate of your chosen currency may fall against the dollar. This can happen if the issuing nation falls on hard times, or chooses to devalue its currency to gain an economic advantage against the dollar. We saw this for many years, as Japan and Switzerland gamed their currencies against the dollar. Similarly, while China may have a massive trade surplus, China does not want its currency to appreciate against the dollar. Keep in mind that these shifts can be large. Don't put a large amount of money in a foreign currency account, unless you are willing to bear a significant drop in the value of your currency against the dollar.

Here's another concern. In countries that suffered a currency collapse, the government often froze, or even seized, foreign currency held in local bank accounts. This was typically done by means of a forced conversion of foreign currency to the local currency. If this were to occur in the United States, then the government could potentially force you to sell your euro or Japanese yen, for dollars, at whatever price the government determines. Thus, as long as your foreign currency account is held in a bank in U.S. jurisdiction, you may not be able to sleep well at night.

As always, make your own decisions regarding what currency you want to purchase, if any, and the amount of your investment.

Online foreign exchange accounts.

Certain companies offer the equivalent of a foreign bank account, through an online platform. Wise – formerly known as TransferWise – is one of the most successful of these services.

Wise allows its customers to hold and manage money in over 40 different currencies. Wise will convert funds between currencies at competitive exchange rates – through the internet – without the need to go to a bank.

Like Everbank, Wise gives its customers an ATM card. You can use that card to withdraw funds – in the local currency – in many countries around the world. Thus, the Wise account is very flexible.

For some currencies, Wise will actually give you a separate bank account number, and the account details, for your account. In other words, for accounts held in these currencies, you can wire money directly to your own account at Wise, without sending the funds through a central bank account.

This can be a major advantage. The account details for these accounts are located at real banks, that are not in the United States.

For example, Wise keeps Canadian dollar accounts in Ottawa, Canada. Euro-denominated accounts are held in Brussels, Belgium. Wise holds accounts in British pounds in London. Thus, you get a measure of protection from a possible U.S. confiscation of the funds.

However, keep in mind that Wise does do business in the United States. Thus, the company is subject to U.S. law, and could possibly be forced to participate in a scheme to confiscate foreign currency, held by American citizens.

The other downside is that Wise is not a bank. Your funds are therefore not protected by FDIC-type programs in the United States, or other countries. Thus, your funds are more at risk, if you keep them at Wise.

Finally, unlike Everbank, Wise pays no interest at all, on funds kept within its internet platform. Thus, Wise can be a short-term solution for converting funds, or providing an emergency place to stash funds outside the dollar. However, I would be careful about using it as a place to park large amounts of money, for a long period of time.

Offshore bank accounts.

We have worked our way up the ladder to offshore bank accounts.

An offshore bank account is an account located in a foreign country, with no apparent connection to the United States.

It is not easy for most Americans to open an offshore bank account.

In 2010, President Obama signed into law the Foreign Account Tax Compliance Act, also known as "FATCA". The law requires foreign financial institutions to report to the Internal Revenue Service information about financial accounts held by U.S. taxpayers.

The act creates a large amount of expense for foreign banks. As a result, many banks simply decided that they would not accept U.S. taxpayers as customers. Thus, about 98% of foreign banks will no longer do business with Americans. The remaining banks want large minimum deposits, to make it worth their time, to deal with the paperwork.

If you are looking for a genuine offshore bank account, where you can keep funds readily available in a different currency, then I would recommend Canada. Many banks in Canada will do business with American citizens, for reasonable deposit amounts. However, to open these accounts, you must travel to Canada. You cannot open a Canadian account at a U.S. branch of a Canadian bank.

The only downside with a Canadian bank, is that your funds are typically kept in Canadian dollars. If the U.S. dollar falls materially, it is likely that the Canadian dollar will drop, as well, due to the loss of Canada's exports to the United States.

However, the Canadian dollar may do better than the U.S. dollar, for several reasons. First, Canada does not have as large a trade deficit as the United States. Second, the Canadian dollar is backed by commodities, such as oil, timber and wheat. These commodities can be sold to countries other than the United States. Canada is already taking steps to diversify its markets. Thus, Canada is a reasonable place to park emergency money, outside of the U.S. dollar.

It is more difficult to get a foreign bank account elsewhere. For example, Mexico will not allow a foreigner to open a bank account, unless the foreigner has residency.

There are some online services that will open an offshore bank account. For example, I am aware of one service that will open accounts in Belize, a former British colony located just south of Mexico. However, be careful about putting large amounts in the banks in Central America. Don't assume that your funds are completely safe. Crime does occur in these nations.

Sometimes funds disappear from these accounts. For example, there is a small community of American expats in San Miguel de Allende, Mexico. Some of these Americans lost money that they deposited in Mexican banks, due to organized crime. Other countries may be safer.

However, keep in mind, you are not dealing with American law. Use your judgment about where to place your funds.

Tactical relocation overseas

In Argentina, the wealthy knew in advance that the peso was going to collapse. They purchased homes across the border, and retreated to these homes when their currency dropped.

Wealthy Americans are already taking a page from this playbook.

During the covid epidemic, billionaire Elon Musk sold all of his real estate located in the United States. Musk sold four mansions in Los Angeles, for a total of $62 million. He also sold a 16,000-square-foot mansion in Hillsborough, California, for nearly $41 million.

In the media, Musk boasted that he had become a "man without a home." So where did Musk go? Is he still living in the United States? The answer is barely. Musk relocated to the Texas side of the Mexican border. He now lives in Boca Chica, Texas, just a short walk from the Gulf of Mexico or the Mexican border. If Musk needed to leave the United States, he could easily slip across the border, or jump on a boat in front of his rocket test facility.

In 2021, actor George Clooney and his wife, Amal, announced that they were moving to France. Clooney told the media that he preferred the quieter pace of life in France.

In 2024, actress Eva Longoria announced that she had emigrated from the United States. Longoria now divides her time between Spain and Mexico, her two primary residences. Longoria denies that she made the move for political reasons.

Singer Britany Spears also moved to Mexico. Spears claims that she moved to escape the U.S. paparazzi. Spears is not the only actress to move abroad to escape the media. In 2014, Lindsay Lohan moved to Dubai for the same reason.

In April 2022, Ellen DeGeneres sold a house that she had owned in Montecito, California for less than a year. DeGeneres and her wife,

Portia de Rossi, emigrated to the Cotswold region of the United Kingdom. In July 2025, DeGeneres put her Cotswold house up for sale. However, she didn't return to the United States. She bought a bigger and more modern house nearby.

In January 2025, Rosie O'Donnell emigrated to Ireland. O'Donnell cited concerns about the political situation in America. A few months later, Richard Gere and his wife, Alejandra, moved to Spain. In July 2025, Nicole Kidman and her husband, Keith Urban, applied for residency in Portugal.

I suspect that these people are moving for more than quality of life reasons. More and more, wealthy Americans are setting up "Plan B." Plan B is the ability to quickly set up a new life, outside of the United States, if life becomes untenable in America. That means having financial resources, a place to stay, and preferably foreign residency.

Foreign residency

For most Americans, getting foreign residency can be difficult. This is because foreign residency is expensive.

Most countries offer something called a "Golden Visa," which provides permanent residency in a foreign country, in return for a payment to the country providing the visa.

Until the covid epidemic, it was possible to obtain residency in Panama by simply opening a bank account for a business in Panama. The total cost to obtain residency was only about $7,000 -- and that included the attorney fee. After covid, Panama raised the price of its visa program. As of October 2024, Panama requires the purchase of least $400,000 of real estate in the country, to obtain residence.

Panama's visa program is now typical of the program offered by the less-expensive countries on the planet. One of the best deals around is Portugal, as Nicole Kidman apparently found. Like Panama, Portugal requires an investment in real estate or a local business. The investment is between €250,000 and €500,000, with additional fees for processing and renewals.

Other countries are much more expensive. For example, to gain residence in England – as did Ellen DeGeneres – the main option is the Tier 1 Investor visa. This requires a minimum investment of £2 million in a qualifying UK company.

Singapore offers a Global Investor Program, for persons who want permanent residency in the country. The program requires a minimum investment of about $2 million U.S. dollars. The investment can be in a Singapore-based business, or in a government-approved investment fund.

Many Americans find Mexico to be a cheaper option, for obtaining foreign residency. To obtain residence in Mexico, you must demonstrate economic solvency, either through passive monthly income, or a minimum balance in a bank or brokerage account.

As of 2025, Mexico required a passive monthly income of about $4,100. Alternatively, one could obtain residence by maintaining about $70,000 in a bank account for twelve consecutive months. These numbers used to be much lower. Like Panama, Mexico increased the numbers significantly after the covid years.

Many Americans look to Canada, as a possible Plan B country. Canada does seek immigrants. However, it seeks young and healthy immigrants to keep health care costs down. Canada uses a point system to decide who gets a visa to live in the country. Applicants between 20 to 29 years of age get the most points. Older applicants, who are well educated or have skills, are also seriously considered. However, if you are over 45, getting in can be difficult, unless you make a large investment in the country.

Foreign real estate

If you are seeking to protect more than $50,000 from a decline in the U.S. dollar, then I would suggest foreign real estate.

Foreign real estate is not an easy game to play. Often, you have to deal with a language barrier. For this reason, you may want to consider property in England.

For many years, Britain has attracted investments from the Middle East and from Hong Kong, due to the English language, transparency of the market, and the benefits of English law.

According to the Wall Street Journal, U.S. buyers are now the largest demographic group of overseas buyers in London. Americans accounted for a quarter of the upmarket purchases in the city in 2024. That was up nearly 20% from the prior year.

According to British real estate broker, Jo Eccles, U.S. buyers traditionally tended to rent for about five years, before putting down roots. Now, she says, they are choosing to buy after only a year.

If you are planning to rent your foreign property, talk to an accountant first. England, for example, does have certain heightened taxes on rents received by foreigners.

If you are looking for foreign real estate – in the English language – closer to home, you might want to consider Canada. Canada has its own hurdles. On January 1, 2023, Canada made it illegal for foreigners, including those from the United States, to purchase smaller properties. These are defined has having one to three dwelling units. Thus, if you want a single-family house in Canada, that won't be possible, unless you have Canadian residency.

Canada imposed this restriction because of a housing shortage. Too many Americans were buying houses in Canada, and leaving them empty. Canada also imposed a vacancy tax, on empty dwelling units. The tax is typically about 1% of the value of the house, per year.

It is still possible for Americans to buy a building with at least four dwelling units, in Canada. Keep in mind that much of Canada uses rent control. Rent control limits the amount a landlord can raise the rent each year. In Canada, the permitted rent increase is often below the known inflation rate. (This is why Canada has a housing shortage.) Thus, an investment in rental real estate in most Canadian provinces could have a limited return.

Canada's ban on foreign purchases is due to expire on January 1, 2027. However, I wouldn't count on the market opening at that time. Canada has previously extended the ban at least once.

Americans looking to protect cash should consider investing in Mexico, the Caribbean, or Latin America. Many of these locations will require doing business in Spanish. However, this can be an easy way to get funds out of the United States, and provide an emergency safe haven – should it become necessary to leave the United States for a period of time.

Conclusion

On the afternoon of April 14, 1912, the weather in the North Atlantic was clear, calm and cold. On that day, J. Bruce Ismay was in excellent spirits. Ismay – the chairman of the White Star Line – was traveling on his company's ship, the Titanic, from England to New York. He was confident that the Titanic would soon break the record for the fastest ship to cross the ocean.

On the evening of April 14, the Titanic entered an area of the North Atlantic known as the "Devil's hole." Numerous ships had sunk in that area, due to the prevalence of ice. This was known to the entire crew, including the maids on board.

Over the course of the day, the Titanic received at least six warnings of ice. Despite these warnings, Ismay told the ship's captain, Edward John Smith, to go full-speed ahead. Smith followed orders, and kept the ship at a rapid pace, as the sun went down. Other ships, such as the Californian, stopped for the night, due to the presence of ice.

Ismay drove the Titanic into an ice field that was twenty miles long, and four miles wide. Directly in front of the Titanic was an iceberg one-hundred feet high, with a mass estimated to be 1.5 million tons. The iceberg was vastly larger than the ship.

Within hours, the Titanic was on the bottom of the ocean. Imagine Ismay's disappointment, when he radioed his shareholders the following morning, and told them that the company's trophy property no longer existed.

This book has compared the U.S. economy to the Titanic. As with the Titanic, the United States is ignoring warning signs. Federal debt levels are now at 120% of GDP. This is a known signal to slow down on the issuance of debt.

That has not happened. Instead, the United States is taking on more debt. We are traveling full-speed into a known hazard. Many would say that the bow of the ship is already underwater, and that the lights are about to go out.

Like the Titanic, we don't have sufficient lifeboats. We have virtually no foreign currency reserves to cushion a drop in the dollar; we have largely emptied our strategic petroleum reserve; we have closed virtually all of our steel mills; we no longer maintain an emergency grain supply; and we have sold off our stockpiles of minerals, meant for national defense. America is dependent upon China for rare earth elements, necessary to produce modern weapons. America is dependent upon foreigners for the clothes we wear, and for much of the food that we eat.

The Chinese and the Russians are laughing at us. "Look at the Americans," they say. "They don't know how to create wealth. They will soon be living in Africa." Meanwhile, China goes from success to success – building factories, high-speed rail, and exporting to the world. China's gold reserves increase every year, while America's stash of gold hasn't grown since 1950.

American policy makers need to understand that shopping malls do not create wealth. We have built an economy that destroys wealth, by consuming the world's goods by means of our control over the world's reserve currency. In the event of a balance of payments crisis, our shopping malls could quickly be looted and empty.

The United States needs to learn from history. During the 20th century, Britain repeatedly devalued its currency to remain competitive. Britain devalued the pound 30% in 1931; another 30% in 1947; and 14% more in 1967. These devaluations helped keep Britain competitive. They avoided a catastrophic collapse of Britain's currency, like those experienced in Lebanon and Argentina.

Whether we like it or not, the world is moving away from the dollar. The decline in the dollar can happen either slowly, as was done in Britain, or it can happen quickly, as happened in Lebanon and Argentina. Increasingly, the BRICS alliance has the ability to collapse the dollar at will. They can do so, either quickly or over time.

The choice is ours. If the United States does not proactively manage the foreseeable decline in the value of the dollar, America could be facing a difficult future.

About the Author

Elliott J. Schuchardt studied political theory at Oxford University, in England, and at Cornell University. In 1993, he graduated from Columbia Law School.

Schuchardt practiced law for nearly three decades. He focused his legal practice on the defense of civil liberties, and governmental policy.

In 2014, Schuchardt sued the U.S. government for collecting the nation's e-mail database without a warrant. In that case, Schuchardt worked with a group of former U.S. intelligence officials, who were seeking to enforce the 4th Amendment.

In 2013, Schuchardt represented a group of students who were seeking to prevent the closing of Sweet Briar College, located in Amherst, Virginia. Schuchardt obtained the injunction that kept the school open.

Between 2018 and 2025, Schuchardt worked to improve due process rights in the Tennessee court system.

Prior to publishing this book, Schuchardt received over 8 million content-views for his posts online, regarding politics, history and the U.S. dollar.

Schuchardt is a candidate for the Tennessee House of Representatives in the 2026 election.

BIBLIOGRAPHY

Assessing and Strengthening the Manufacturing and Defense Industrial Base and Supply Chain Resiliency of the United States (U.S. Government Printing Office, Sept. 2018).

Daron Acemoglo & James A. Robinson, Why Nations Fail: The Origins of Power, Prosperity, and Poverty (Crown Business, 2012).

Fernando Aguirre, The Modern Survival Manual: Surviving the Economic Collapse (Self Published, 2009).

C. Fred Bergsten and Joseph E. Gagnon, Currency Conflict and Trade Policy: A New Strategy for the United States (Peterson Institute for International Economics, 2017).

C. Fred Bergstein, Dilemmas of the Dollar: The Economics and Politics of United States International Monetary Policy (Routledge 1996).

C. Fred Bergsten, Towards a New International Economic Order: Selected Papers of C. Fred Bergsten, 1972-1974 (Lexington Books, 1975).

C. Fred Bergstein, The United States in the World Economy: Selected Papers of C. Fred Bergstein: 1981-1982 (Lexington Books, 1983).

Peter L. Bernstein, The Power of Gold: The History of an Obsession (John Wiley & Sons, 2000).

Paul Blustein, And The Money Kept Rolling In (And Out): The World Bank, Wall Street, The IMF, and the Bankrupting of Argentina (Public Affairs, 2005).

Anthony Cave Brown, Oil, God & Gold: The Story of Aramco and the Saudi Kings (Houghton Mifflin Co., 1999).

Ray Dalio, Principles for Navigating Big Debt Crises (Self Published, 2018).

Alec Cairncross & Barry Eichengreen, Sterling in Decline (Palgrave Macmillan, 1983).

Fabian Calvo, The Global Economic Reset: The Day America Loses the World Reserve Currency (Self Published, 2014).

William R. Clark, Petrodollar Warfare: Oil, Iraq and the Future of the U.S. Dollar (New Society Publishers, 2005)

Philip Coggan, Paper Promises: Debt, Money and The New World Order (Penguin Group, 2012).

Jared Diamond, Collapse: How Societies Choose to Fail or Succeed (Viking Publishers, 2005).

Barry Eichengreen, Exorbitant Privilege: The Rise and Fall of the Dollar and the Future of the International Monetary System (Oxford University Press, 2011).

James Fallows, Looking at the Sun: The Rise of the New East Asian Economic and Political System (Pantheon Books, 1994).

John Galtung, The Fall of the U.S. Empire – And Then What? (Transcend University Press, 2009).

Benjamin Graham, World Commodities & World Currency (McGraw Hill, 1944).

G. Edward Griffin, The Creature From Jekyll Island: A Second Look at the Federal Reserve (American Media, 2002).

Philip Haslam and Russell Lamberti, When Money Destroys Nations: How Hyperinflation Ruined Zimbabwe, How Ordinary People Survived, and Warnings for Nations that Print Money (Penguin Group, 2015).

Paul Kennedy, The Rise and Fall of the Great Powers: Economic Change and Military Conflict From 1500 to 2000 (Random House, 1987).

James Howard Kunstler, Living in the Long Emergency: Global Crisis, the Failure of the Futurists, and the Early Adapters Who Are Showing Us the Way Forward (Ben Bella Books, 2020).

Fadi Lama, Why the West Can't Win: From Bretton Woods to a Multipolar World (Clarity Press, 2023).

Qiao Lang & Wang Xiangsui, Unrestricted Warfare: China's Master Plan to Destroy America (Filament Books, 2004).

Robert Lekachman, The Age of Keynes (Random House, 1966). Robert Lighthizer, No Trade is Free: Changing Course, Taking on China, and Helping America's Workers (Broadside Books, 2023).

Friedrich List, The National System of Political Economy (Pantianos Classics, 1841).

Andrei Martyanov, Disintegration: Indicators of the Coming American Collapse (Clarity Press, 2021).

Andrei Martyanov, Losing Military Supremacy: The Myopia of American Strategic Planning (Clarity Press, 2018).

Daniel McDowell, Bucking the Buck: U.S. Financial Sanctions and the International Backlash Against the Dollar (Oxford University Press, 2023).

Chris Miller, Chip War: The Fight for the World's Most Critical Technology (Scribner, 2022).

Dmitry Orlov, Reinventing Collapse: The Soviet Experience and American Prospects (New Society Publishers, 2011).

Dmitry Orlov, Societies That Collapse: Essays (Self Published, 2014).

Ivo Maes & Ilaria Pasotti, Robert Triffin: A Life (Oxford University Press, 2021).

Michael Pillsbury, The Hundred-Year Marathon: China's Secret Strategy to Replace America as the Global Superpower (Henry Holt & Co. 2015).

Clyde Prestowitz, The Betrayal of American Prosperity: Free Market Delusions, America's Decline, and How We Must Compete in the Post-Dollar Era (Free Press, 2010).

James Rickards, The Big Drop: How to Grow Your Wealth During the Coming Collapse (Laissez Faire Books, 2016).

Godfrey Roberts, Why China Leads the World (Ingram Books, 2023).

Jim Rohwer, Asia Rising: Why America Will Prosper as Asia's Economies Boom (Simon & Schuster, 1995).

Cheryl Schonardt-Bailey, From the Corn Laws to Free Trade: Interests, Ideas and Institutions in Historical Perspective (M.I.T. Press, 2006).

Jerome L. Smith, The Coming Currency Collapse and What You Can Do About It (Griffin Publishing, 1980).

David E. Spiro, The Hidden Hand of American Hegemony (Cornell University Press, 1999).

Ben Steil, The Battle of Bretton Woods: John Maynard Keynes, Harry Dexter White, and the Making of a New Money Order (Princeton University Press, 2013).

John B. Taylor, Reform of the International Monetary System: Why and How? (MIT Press, 2019).

Robert Triffin, Europe and the Money Muddle: From Bilateralism to Near Convertibility, 1947-1956 (Oxford University Press, 1957).

Robert Triffin, "The Future of the European Payments System," (May 1958), in International Trade and Finance: A collection of Wicksell Lectures: 1958-1964 (Almqvist & Wicksell, 1965).

Robert Triffin, Gold and the Dollar Crisis (Yale University Press, 1960).

Robert Triffin et al., Maintaining and Restoring Balance in International Payments (Princeton University Press, 1966).

Robert Triffin, Our International Monetary System: Yesterday, Today and Tomorrow (Random House, 1968).

Robert Triffin, The World Money Maze: National Currencies in International Payments (Yale University Press, 1966).

Andrew Dickson White, Fiat Money Inflation in France (Public domain, 1914).

www.ingramcontent.com/pod-product-compliance
Lightning Source LLC
Chambersburg PA
CBHW070615030426
42337CB00020B/3813